3/98

VGM's HANDBOOK *of* HEALTH CARE CAREERS

edited by Carla S. Rogers, Ph.D.

VGM Career Horizons
NTC/Contemporary Publishing Company

Library of Congress Cataloging-in-Publication Data is available from the United States Library of Congress.

Published by VGM Career Horizons
An imprint of NTC/Contemporary Publishing Company
4255 West Touhy Avenue, Lincolnwood (Chicago), Illinois 60646-1975 U.S.A.
Manufactured in the United States of America
International Standard Book Number: 0-8442-4148-2
18 17 16 15 14 13 12 11 10 9 8 7 6 5 4 3 2 1

Contents

Part II How to Get and Keep a Job in Health Care

The Paperwork

The Interview

Health Careers in the 21st Century

How to Use This Book

VGM's Handbook of Health Care Careers contains vital information on popular careers in health care. In Part I of this book, health care careers have been organized into major categories such as Medicine, Allied Health, Dentistry, Eye Care, Animal Care, and Research and Education. This categorization will make it easier for you to refer to the section of your interest. Each career has been carefully researched and described in text that is easy to understand. Every career is described in the following fashion:

- *The Job.* A general description of the job and the major responsibilities.
- *Places of Employment and Working Conditions.* Includes where major employers in the field are located and the type of work environment you can expect, i.e., office work, outdoor work, urban or rural location. Typical working hours are also listed.
- *Qualifications, Education, and Training.* Includes the specifics on degrees necessary, qualifications and skills, and special training you will need to get a job in that field.
- *Potential and Advancement.* Contains the approximate number of persons employed in the field nationwide, projections on growth, and typical pathways for advancement or promotion.
- *Income.* The most current salaries available, for beginners and experienced workers in the field. Keep in mind that these figures are constantly changing, due primarily to supply and demand within the labor force and to inflation. Be sure to check with employers and associations for salary updates.
- *Additional Sources of Information.* Names and address of associations and other groups that can supply additional information about careers in that field. These organizations can be very helpful; don't hesitate to contact them if you need additional information.

Part I of this book allows you to compare and contrast various careers in health care, all within one volume. You can use it to find out information about careers that interest you, or you can read it cover to cover to explore a variety of career paths that you may find appealing.

Part II of this book contains important chapters concerning getting a job in the competitive health care industry. These chapters will help you with interviews, resumes, cover letters, and application forms. An additional chapter on health care in the 21st century will keep you updated on the changing health care industry.

VGM's
HANDBOOK
of
HEALTH CARE
CAREERS

Part I

The Careers

Medicine

Allopathic Physician (M.D.)
Osteopathic Physician (D.O.)
Physician Assistant
Chiropractor
Medical Assistant
Medical Record Technician
Medical Secretary
Health Services Manager
Podiatrist
Prosthetist and Orthotist
Psychiatrist
Psychologist

Medicine   Careers in medicine require commitment, dedication, integrity, and a desire to help people of all races and backgrounds. These careers are demanding, but very rewarding. From the physician to the assistant to the office manager, each career offers satisfaction, a sense of self-worth, and an opportunity to make a difference. Each career involves the prevention and curing of disease of some part of the human body, aiding in symptom control, or just being a part of a medical team devoted to health care.

Careers included in this section are: allopathic physician, osteopathic physician, physician assistant, chiropractor, medical assistant, medical secretary, medical records technician, health services manager, podiatrist, prosthetist and orthotist, psychiatrist, and psychologist.

Allopathic Physician (M.D.)

There are two types of physicians: the M.D.—Doctor of Medicine—also known as "allopathic" physician; and the D.O.—Doctor of Osteopathic Medicine—also know as osteopathic physician. Both have similar duties.

The Job   Physicians diagnose diseases, treat illnesses and injuries, and are involved in research, rehabilitation, and preventive medicine.

Most physicians specialize in a particular field of medicine, such as emergency medicine, obstetrics/gynecology, neurology, pathology, radiology, anesthesiology, orthopedic surgery, internal medicine, general surgery, psychiatry, or pediatrics. The fastest-growing speciality is family medicine, which emphasizes general medicine.

Most new physicians open their own offices or join associate or group practices. Those who enter the armed forces start with the rank of captain in the army or air force or lieutenant in the navy. Other federal positions are in the Department of Veterans Affairs; the U.S. Public Health Service; and the Department of Health and Human Services.

Places of Employment and Working Conditions   Just about every community has at least one physician.

The northeastern states have the highest ratios of physicians to population; the southern states have the lowest. Physicians tend to locate in urban areas

5

close to hospital facilities and educational centers; rural areas are often underserved.

Many physicians have long and irregular working hours. Specialists work fewer hours than general practitioners. Physicians do have the option of curtailing their practices as they grow older, thus being able to work at a reduced pace past the normal retirement age.

Most physicians work in private offices, clinics, and group practices. Some work in hospitals as full-time staff members, or residents. Others work in public health, federal agencies, and medical colleges.

Qualifications, Education, and Training

Anyone interested in this field must have a strong desire to serve the sick and injured. He or she must have emotional stability and the ability to make quick decisions in an emergency and be able to relate well to people. The study of medicine is long and expensive and requires a commitment to intense, vigorous training and long years of classroom and clinical study.

High school should include as much mathematics and science as possible, and grades should average B or above.

It takes eleven to thirteen years to become a physician: four years of undergraduate school, four years of medical school, and three to five years of residency training. Further specialization, for example plastic surgery, may take seven to eight years of residency!

Most medical school applicants have a bachelor's degree, although medical schools will occasionally accept three years of premedical college study. Competition for entrance into medical school is fierce. Premedical college grades of B or better are usually necessary, along with a high grade on the Medical College Admission Test (MCAT). Other relevant factors are the applicant's character, personality, and leadership qualities; medical experience; letters of recommendation; and, in state-supported medical schools, areas of residence.

It usually takes four years to complete medical school; students with outstanding ability sometimes complete it in three. A few schools have programs that allow completion of premedical and medical studies in a total of six years.

The first half of medical school is spent in classrooms and laboratories studying medical sciences. The remaining time is spent in clinical work under the supervision of experienced physicians. At the completion of medical school, students are awarded a doctor of medicine (M.D.) degree.

After graduation, a three-year hospital residency is usually completed. Those seeking certification in a specialty spend up to five years in advanced residency training; this is followed by two or more years of practice in the speciality before the required specialty board examination is taken.

Physicians who intend to teach or do research must earn a master's or Ph.D. degree in a field such as biochemistry or microbiology.

All physicians must be licensed to practice medicine. Requirements usually include graduation from an accredited medical school, completion of a residency program, and a passing grade on a licensing examination—usually the National Board of Medical Examiners (NBME) test. This examination consists of three parts. Part I is taken after the two basic science years. Part II is taken following clinical rotations. Part III is taken after completing an internship year. Physicians licensed in one state can obtain a license in some other states without further examination.

Graduates of foreign medical schools must pass an examination given by the Educational Commission for Foreign Medical Graduates before they are allowed to serve a residency in the United States.

Potential and Advancement

As of 1996, there were about 736,279 physicians in the United States. Of these, 580,130 were men, and 156,149 were women. Employment opportunities should be very good through the year 2000 due to the growing demands for health care. New technologies, increases in treatable illnesses, and increases in available tests and procedures will increase the need for physicians. Baby boomers will need more health care as they age. Anticipated increases in the number of medical graduates of existing and new U.S. medical schools, combined with foreign medical graduates, could cause the supply to exceed the demand. This should encourage more physicians to establish practices in areas that have traditionally lacked sufficient medical services such as rural and inner-city areas. An increase in the supply of new physicians will also mean more competition in some speciality fields. Primary care practitioners, such as family physicians, pediatricians, and internal medicine specialists, will continue to be in demand.

Income

According to the American Medical Association, average income for allopathic physicians was $189,300 in 1993. Earnings for physicians will most likely drop in the next decade due to increases in federal policies, HMOs, and managed care combined with decreases in physician reimbursement for treatments and procedures.

New physicians setting up their own practices usually have a few very lean years in the beginning, but once a practice is established, earnings rise rapidly. However, over 80 percent of medical students owe tens of thousands of dollars in school loans. (The estimated average debt for 1994 was $70,000.) Physicians in private practice usually earn more than those in salaried positions, and specialists earn considerably more than general practitioners.

Earnings may vary according to the number of years in practice, geographic region, hours worked, and personality and professional reputation. Salaries also vary considerably according to specialty. For example, median net income of a pediatrician was $120,000 in 1993. That of a radiologist was $240,000.

Because practitioners in metropolitan areas have much better incomes than those in rural areas, some rural communities offer a guaranteed annual income to a physician who is willing to practice in their area.

Additional Sources of Information

American Medical Association (AMA)
535 North Dearborn Street
Chicago, IL 60610

Association of American Medical Colleges (AAMC)
Publications Department
One Dupont Circle, NW, Suite 200
Washington, DC 20036

Osteopathic Physician

The Job   The dictionary defines osteopathy as "a system of medical practice based on the theory that diseases are due chiefly to a loss of structural integrity in the tissues and that this integrity can be restored by manipulation of the parts, supported by the use of medicines, surgery, proper diet, and other therapy." While both M.D.s and D.O.s use all methods of treatment, including drugs and surgery, D.O.s place special emphasis on the human body's ability to heal itself. M.D.s and D.O.s differ primarily in their philosophy of medicine. D.O.s believe good health requires proper alignment of bones, muscles, ligaments, tendons, and nerves. But for all practical purposes, the two types of physicians are almost identical.

Most osteopathic physicians are family doctors engaged in general practice. They see patients at their offices or make house calls and treat patients in osteopathic and other private and public hospitals. Some osteopathic physicians specialize in such fields as internal medicine, neurology, psychiatry, ophthalmology, pediatrics, anesthesiology, physical medicine and rehabilitation, dermatology, obstetrics and gynecology, pathology, proctology, radiology, and surgery.

Most osteopathic physicians are in private practice, although a few hold salaried positions in private industry or government agencies. Others hold full-time positions with osteopathic hospitals and colleges where they are engaged in teaching, research, and writing, as well as health care.

Places of Employment and Working Conditions

Most osteopathic physicians practice in states that have osteopathic hospital facilities; over half are in Florida, Michigan, Pennsylvania, New Jersey, Ohio, Texas, and Missouri. Most general practitioners are located in towns and cities having less than 50,000 people; specialists are usually located in larger cities.

Most D.O.s work more than fifty hours a week. Long, irregular hours during nights, weekends, and holidays are also common. D.O.s who are "on call" make many visits to the hospital.

Qualifications, Education, and Training

Anyone interested in becoming an osteopathic physician should have emotional stability, patience, tact, and the interest and ability to deal effectively with people.

The education requirements for the doctor of osteopathy (D.O.) degree include a minimum of three years of college (although most applicants have a bachelor's degree) plus a three- to four-year professional program. The education and training of an osteopathic physician is very expensive due primarily to the length of time involved. Federal and private funds are available for loans, and federal scholarships are available to those who qualify and agree to a minimum of two years of service for the federal government after completion of training.

Undergraduate study must include courses in chemistry, physics, biology, and English, with high grades an important factor for acceptance into the professional programs. In addition to high grades, schools require a good score on the Medical College Admission Test (MCAT) and letters of recommendation. One very important qualification is the applicant's desire to study osteopathy rather than some other field of medicine.

During the first half of the professional program, the student studies basic sciences such as anatomy, physiology, and pathology as well as as the principles of osteopathy. The second half of the program consists primarily of clinical experience. After graduation, a 12-month internship is usually completed at one of the osteopathic hospitals approved for internship or residency by the American Osteopathic Association. Those who intend to specialize must complete an additional two to five years of training.

All practicing osteopathic physicians must be licensed. State licensing requirements vary, but all states require graduation from an approved school of osteopathic medicine and a passing grade on a state board examination. Most states require an internship at an approved hospital.

Potential and Advancement

There are about 53,500 practicing osteopathic physicians in the United States. Population growth, an increase in the number of persons covered by medical insurance, and the establishment of additional osteopathic hospitals will contribute to an increasing demand for osteopathic physicians. The greatest demand will continue to be in states where osteopathic medicine is well known and accepted as a form of treatment.

Opportunities for new practitioners are best in rural areas (many localities lack medical practitioners of any kind), small towns, and suburbs of large cities. The availability of osteopathic hospital facilities should be considered when one is selecting a location for practice.

Income As is usually the case in any field where setting up an individual practice is the norm, earnings in the first few years are low. Income usually rises substantially once the practice becomes established, and, in the case of osteopathic physicians, is very high in comparison with other professionals. Geographic location and the income level of the community are also factors that affect the level of income. The average annual income of general practitioners is similar to that of an M.D. The median net income of all physicians was $156,000 in 1993.

Additional Sources of Information

American Association of Colleges of Osteopathic Medicine
6110 Executive Boulevard, Suite 405
Rockville, MD 20852

American Osteopathic Association
Department of Public Relations
142 East Ontario Street
Chicago, IL 60611

Physician Assistant

The Job Physician assistants, or PAs, relieve primary care physicians of some of their duties. They are trained to perform such medical procedures as taking medical histories, performing physical examinations, making preliminary diagnoses, prescribing treatments, and suggesting medications and drug therapies. In some states, PAs are permitted to prescribe medication.

PAs also treat minor medical problems such as cuts and burns, and suture, splint, and cast minor injuries. They provide pre- and postoperative care and sometimes assist in surgery. PAs also record progress notes, instruct and counsel patients, and order or carry out therapeutic procedures. Some have managerial duties and order medical and laboratory supplies and equipment. PAs also supervise technicians and assistants.

PAs work in several medical specialties, including family practice, internal medicine, general and thoracic surgery, emergency medicine, and pediatrics.

Other titles for PAs include MEDEX, surgeon's assistant, child health associate, and physician associate.

Places of Employment and Working Conditions PAs work in physicians' offices, hospitals, and clinics. Most PAs work under the supervision of a physician. Some work in inner-city or rural clinics where a physician comes only once or twice a week. The rest of the week, the PA independently provides health care services after consulting with the supervising physician by telephone.

PAs have varying schedules depending on their work setting. Usually they share the same work hours as their supervising physician. If their employer provides 24-hour medical care, they may be required to work nights, weekends, and holidays.

PAs generally work in a comfortable, well-lighted, sanitary environment, but this also depends on the type and location of the work.

Qualifications, Education, and Training PAs should enjoy working with people. Leadership skills, confidence, and emotional stability are also important qualities.

Almost all states require that PAs complete an accredited formal education program. In 1995 there were 61 educational programs for physician assistants. Thirty-seven offer a bachelor's degree; the rest offer a certificate, an associate's degree, or a master's degree. There are currently three programs for surgeon's assistants.

Admission requirements for many programs include two years of college and work experience in the health field. A number of programs, however, are doing away with requirements for previous work experience.

PA programs are usually two years long. They are offered by medical schools, schools of allied health, and four-year colleges; a few are sponsored by community colleges or hospitals. Course work includes classroom instruction and supervised experience in clinical practice.

As of 1995, 49 states had laws concerning the qualifications or practice of PAs and require them to pass a certifying exam given only to graduates of accredited programs. Only those successfully completing the exam may use the credential "Physician Assistant—Certified (PA-C)." To remain certified, PAs must have one-hundred hours of continuing education every two years. They must pass a recertification exam every six years.

Potential and Advancement　In 1994, there were about 56,000 physician assistants. There should be very good opportunities for physician assistants through the year 2005. The health services industry is expected to expand greatly, and PAs will be in demand to relieve doctors of some of their more routine tasks and assist them in more complex medical and surgical procedures.

PAs sometimes advance by taking additional training that allows them to work in a specialty area such as surgery and emergency medicine. Others earn higher salaries and are given more responsibility as they gain experience and increase their knowledge. PAs, though, are always supervised by doctors.

Income　In 1994, the average minimum salary for physician assistants was about $37,639 a year. Experienced physician assistants earned an average salary of about $57,005. Some can earn upwards of $65,000. Income varies by geographic location, years of experience, and specialty.

Additional Sources of Information

American Academy of Physician Assistants
950 North Washington Street
Alexandria, VA 22314

American Medical Association
535 North Dearborn Street
Chicago, IL 60610

Chiropractor

The Job　Chiropractors diagnose and treat patients by manual manipulations (called adjustments) of parts of the body, primarily of musculature, nervous, and skeletal systems—especially the spinal column. This system of treatment is based on the theory that pressure on nerves that pass from the spinal cord to different parts of the body interferes with nerve impulses and their functioning, causing disorders in parts of the body. By means of certain manipulations of the vertebrae, the chiropractor seeks to relieve the pressure on specific nerves and thus remove the cause of a specific ailment.

Most chiropractors also employ x-rays to aid in locating the source of an ailment. They use supplementary treatment with water, light, or heat therapy and may prescribe diet, exercise, and rest. Chiropractors' approach to health care is holistic, using natural, drugless, nonsurgical health treatments.

Newly licensed chiropractors often start their careers by working in salaried positions—as assistants to established practitioners or in chiropractic clinics.

Since a chiropractic practice can be conducted on a part-time basis, it is a good field for people with family responsibilities.

Places of Employment and Working Conditions
Chiropractors often locate in small communities, with about half of all chiropractors practicing in cities of 50,000 or less. California, Oregon, Colorado, Wyoming, Arizona, and New Mexico have the most chiropractors.

Most chiropractors are in private practice, which allows them to schedule their own working hours. Evening and weekend hours are sometimes necessary to accommodate their patients. Some chiropractors are employed by HMOs or are employed by chiropractic college hospitals to do research.

Qualifications, Education, and Training
Manual dexterity rather than strength is necessary for a chiropractor. A keen sense of observation, an ability to deal with people, and a sympathetic manner with the sick are also important.

High school courses in science are important, and the two years of college required before entrance into chiropractic school must include chemistry, biology, physics, English, social sciences, and psychology. Many applicants to chiropractic colleges have bachelor's degrees.

There are 15 chiropractic colleges that are accredited by the Council on Chiropractic Education; two others are working toward accreditation. The four-year course of study emphasizes courses in manipulation and spinal adjustment, but most schools also offer a broad curriculum that includes basic and clinical sciences.

The first two years of study include classroom and laboratory work in anatomy, physiology, and biochemistry. The last two years stress courses in skeletal manipulation and spinal adjustments and provide clinical experience in physical and laboratory diagnosis, neurology, orthopedics, geriatrics, physiotherapy, and nutrition. The degree of D.C. (doctor of chiropractic) is awarded upon completion of the course.

All chiropractors must be licensed to practice. In addition to a state board examination, licensing requirements usually include two years of college and the successful completion of an accredited four-year chiropractic course, as described above. Some states also require a basic science examination. To maintain licensure, almost all states require completion of a specific number of hours of continued education each year.

Potential and Advancement   There are about 36,000 practicing chiropractors. This number will increase because the profession is gaining greater public acceptance. Enrollment in chiropractic colleges has increased in recent years. New chiropractors may find it increasingly difficult to establish a practice in areas where other practitioners are located; the best opportunities will be in areas with few established chiropractors.

Job Outlook   Employment of chiropractors is expected to grow faster than the average for all occupations through the year 2005. Demand for chiropractic services will increase with increases in the older population.

Income   As in any type of independent practice, earnings are relatively low in the beginning but increase as a practice grows. In 1994, median income for chiropractors was about $75,000 after expenses, according to the American Chiropractic Association.

Additional Sources of Information

American Chiropractic Association
1701 Clarendon Boulevard
Arlington, VA 22209

Council on Chiropractic Education
4401 Westown Parkway, Suite 120
West Des Moines, IA 50265

Medical Assistant

The Job   Medical assistants perform administrative tasks and work with patients, helping doctors keep their practices running efficiently.

Medical assistants' duties vary from office to office, depending on the size of the medical practice. In smaller practices, they have a wider range of responsibilities, often performing both administrative and clinical tasks. In larger practices, they may specialize in a particular area. Medical assistants should not be confused with physician assistants.

Laws regarding the procedures medical assistants are permitted to perform vary from state to state, but some of the more common clinical tasks they are allowed to do include taking and recording medical histories and vital signs; explaining treatments to patients; preparing patients for examination; and assisting in examinations.

After an examination, medical assistants may collect laboratory specimens and perform basic laboratory tests; dispose of contaminated supplies; and sterilize medical instruments.

Some of the administrative duties medical assistants often have include answering telephones, greeting patients, recording and filing medical records, filling out insurance forms, scheduling appointments, arranging for hospital admission and laboratory tests, and taking care of billing and bookkeeping.

Medical assistants can also maintain and purchase medical instruments, equipment, and supplies and administer basic patient care, such as removing sutures or drawing blood. Some medical assistants specialize in a certain branch of medicine such as podiatry or ophthalmology.

Places of Employment and Working Conditions   Most medical assistants work in doctors' offices; some work in the offices of optometrists, podiatrists, and chiropractors. Others work in hospitals.

Medical assistants usually have a forty-hour workweek, which may include some weekend and evening hours.

Qualifications, Education, and Training   Medical assistants spend a great deal of time working with people, so they must be neat, pleasant, and courteous. They must be able to listen and follow doctors' instructions closely and also listen to patients' needs.

There are no formal education requirements for medical assistants, and many receive their training on the job. However, formal programs in medical assisting are offered at secondary and postsecondary levels in technical high schools, vocational schools, community and junior colleges, and universities. Most doctors prefer to hire medical assistants with formal training.

Two agencies accredit medical assisting programs: the American Medical Association's Committee on Allied Health Education and Accreditation (CAHEA) and the Accrediting Bureau of Health Education Schools (ABHES). These programs usually include course work in biological sciences and medical terminology and typing, transcription, recordkeeping, accounting, and insurance processing.

There are no general licensing requirements for medical assistants, but some states require passing a test or completing a course for medical assistants who perform certain procedures such as taking x-rays, drawing blood, or giving injections.

Several associations certify or register medical assistants who meet their requirements. Employers often prefer to hire those who are certified and have experience.

Potential and Advancement
There are about 206,000 medical assistants. Job opportunities should be very good through the year 2005 due to the increasing demands for medical care. Seven in ten jobs are in physicians' offices.

Opportunities will be excellent for those with formal training, experience, or both. Those who are certified and have computer and word processing skills will have even greater advantages when seeking employment.

Medical assistants may advance by becoming office managers. Others become consultants for medical office management or for the medical insurance industry. Some work for hospitals as ward clerks, medical record clerks, phlebotomists, and EKG technicians. Others sometimes get further education and become nurses or work in some field of medical technology.

Income
Earnings for medical assistants vary widely depending on the worker's credentials and level of experience, the size and location of the employer, and the number of hours worked. A 1995 survey by the Health Care Group showed that the average hourly wages for medical assistants with less than two years of experience ranged from $7.51 to $10.50. A medical assistant with more than five years of experience can earn from $9.60 to $13.12 per hour. Wages tend to be higher in the West and the Northeast.

Additional Sources of Information

The American Association of Medical Assistants
20 North Wacker Drive, Suite 1575
Chicago, IL 60606-2903

Registered Medical Assistants of American Medical Technologists
710 Higgins Road
Park Ridge, IL 60068-5765

Accrediting Bureau of Health Education Schools
2700 South Quincy Street, Suite 210
Arlington, VA 22206

Medical Record Technician

The Job   Medical record technicians are responsible for keeping an accurate permanent file on patients treated by doctors and hospitals.

When patients are undergoing treatment, doctors and hospitals keep records of their medical history, results of physical exams, x-ray and lab test reports, diagnoses and treatments, and doctors' and nurses' notes. Also included is information about the patients' symptoms, the tests undergone, and the response to treatment. These are very important legal documents.

Medical record technicians assemble, organize, and check these records for completeness and accuracy. Often doctors and nurses record their information and observations on computer, and medical record technicians must retrieve them from the hospital's central computer.

After medical record technicians have gathered all of the information, they consult classification manuals and assign codes to the diagnoses and procedures included in the record. They then assign the patient to a diagnosis-related group (DRG), which determines the amount the hospital will be reimbursed by Medicare or other insurance programs that use the DRG system.

The medical records that technicians keep serve several important purposes. They are also important for documentation in the case of legal actions and for insurance claims and Medicare reimbursement.

Medical record technicians sometimes analyze data and provide statistics that help hospital administrators and planners keep the hospital running efficiently, improve patient care, or respond to surveys. Tumor registrars compile and maintain all records of cancer patients in order to provide essential information for research studies and physicians.

Medical record technicians also sometimes collect and interpret medical records for law firms, insurance companies, government agencies, researchers, and patients.

A person who supervises all medical record clerks and transcribers and manages the medical record department is called a medical record administrator.

Places of Employment and Working Conditions
Most medical record technicians work in hospitals; others work in medical group practices, HMOs, nursing homes, clinics, and other facilities that deliver health care.

Medical record technicians usually work a 40-hour week, with some overtime. Often they work day, evening, or night shifts because hospital medical record offices operate 18 to 24 hours a day. There is little or no patient contact.

Medical record technicians usually work in comfortable environments, but the work can be stressful because of the necessity for accuracy and close attention to detail.

Qualifications, Education, and Training
Medical record technicians who have earned the credential *accredited record technician* are generally preferred by employers. To become accredited, medical record technicians must pass a written examination given by the American Medical Record Association (AMRA). The requirement for taking the test is the completion of a two-year associate's degree program accredited by the Committee on Allied Health Education and Accreditation in collaboration with AMRA or the independent study program in medical record technology along with 30 semester hours in prescribed areas.

Medical record technology programs include course work in the biological sciences, medical terminology, medical record science, business management, legal aspects, and introduction to computer data processing.

Potential and Advancement
There are about 81,000 medical record technicians, and opportunities should be excellent for those who have completed a formal training program through the year 2005, primarily because of the important role they play in managing health care costs. Due to both growth in the number of medical tests, treatments, and procedures, and the increased importance of medical records to the courts, third-party payers, and consumers, employment possibilities will increase. The need will be greatest in the offices and clinics of doctors, as well as in health maintenance organizations, nursing homes, and home health agencies.

There are three major routes for advancement for medical record technicians—teaching, managing, or specializing. Experienced technicians who have a master's degree in a related field sometimes go into teaching. They can also advance into the management of a medical record department. Finally, technicians can advance into a specialty such as Medicare coding and tumor registry.

Income   According to a 1994 survey, the median annual salary for medical record technicians was $36,700. The average annual salary for a medical record technician with the federal government was $23,779 in 1995.

Additional Sources of Information

American Medical Record Association
875 North Michigan Avenue, Suite 1850
John Hancock Center
Chicago, IL 60611

American Health Information Management Association
919 N. Michigan Ave., Suite 1400
Chicago, IL 60611

Medical Secretary

The Job   Secretaries are the center of communication in an office. The duties they perform keep offices running efficiently. Medical secretaries are specialized secretaries who are employed by physicians or medical scientists.

Medical secretaries transcribe dictation, type letters, and help doctors or medical scientists prepare reports, speeches, and articles. They may record medical histories, arrange for hospitalization, and order supplies.

They also have responsibilities similar to other secretaries. They take shorthand, deal with visitors, keep track of appointments, make travel arrangements, and take care of the employer's paperwork. Secretaries operate office equipment such as FAX machines, photocopiers, telephones with voice mail, and computers. They use computers for word processing, running spreadsheets, database management, desktop publishing, and graphics.

Places of Employment and Working Conditions   Medical secretaries are employed throughout the country, in physicians' offices, hospitals, and other types of health agencies. They may also be employed in academic institutions, such as medical or dental schools.

Working conditions vary, but full-time medical secretaries usually work a 37- to 40-hour week.

Qualifications, Education, and Training

Medical secretaries must be accurate and neat. They must display discretion and initiative and have a good command of spelling, grammar, punctuation, and vocabulary. They need to know medical terms and be familiar with hospital or laboratory procedures.

High school business courses are valuable as well as college preparatory courses, because secretaries should have a good general background. People interested in this field should take as many English courses as possible.

Secretarial training as part of a college education or at a private business school is preferred by many employers. Training for specialty areas such as medicine can take a year or two.

Well-trained and highly experienced secretaries may qualify for the designation *certified professional secretary* (CPS) by passing a series of examinations given by the National Secretaries Association. This is a mark of achievement in the secretarial field and is recognized as such by many employers.

Potential and Advancement

The demand for well-qualified medical secretaries will continue to grow as demand for medical services increases. Job opportunities should be very good through the year 2005.

Opportunities for advancement depend on the acquisition of new or improved skills and on increasing knowledge of the medical field. Some medical secretaries may become administrative assistants or office managers.

Retraining and continuing education may be important to the job, as well as to advancement. Classes to operate new equipment may be essential.

Income

Salaries for medical secretaries vary greatly depending on the level of their skill, experience, and responsibility; the area of the country in which they work; and the type of employer they have.

The average annual salary for all types of secretaries was $26,700 in 1993, with a range from $19,100 to $38,400. Secretaries working in the West and Midwest earn higher salaries in general than those working in the Northeast and South.

Additional Source of Information

Professional Secretaries International
301 East Armour Boulevard
Kansas City, MO 64111

Health Services Manager

The Job   The exact title may vary from institution to institution, but the responsibilities are the same—to plan, organize, coordinate, and supervise the delivery of health care. There are two types of health services managers: generalists, who manage or help to manage an entire facility; and health specialists, who manage specific clinical departments or services found only in the health industry.

The top administrator must staff the hospital with both medical and non-medical personnel; provide all aspects of patient care services; purchase supplies and equipment; plan space allocations; and arrange for housekeeping services such as laundry, security, and maintenance. The administrator must also provide and work within a budget; act as liaison between the directors of the hospital and the medical staff; keep up with developments in the health care field including government regulations; handle hospital community relations; and sometimes act as a fund-raiser. Their knowledge must include business as well as developments in clinical areas.

In large facilities, the administrator has a staff of assistants with expertise in a variety of fields, but in small and medium-sized institutions, the administrator is responsible for all of them.

Health specialists manage the daily operations of individual, specialized departments such as surgery, rehabilitation therapy, nursing, and medical records. These workers have more narrowly defined responsibilities than generalists. They also receive more specialized training and experience in their field.

Depending on the size of the institution, a new graduate might start as an administrative assistant, an assistant administrator, a specialist in a specific management area, a department head, or an assistant department head. In a small health care facility, the new graduate would start in a position with broad responsibilities, while in a large hospital the position might be narrow in scope with rotating work in several departments necessary to gain broad experience.

Places of Employment and Working Conditions   Health services managers work throughout the country in hospitals and health care facilities of all sizes. In addition, health services managers are employed by nursing homes and extended care facilities, community health centers, mental health centers, outreach clinics, city or county health departments, and HMOs. Others are employed as advisors and specialists by insurance companies, government regulatory agencies, and professional standards organizations such as the American Cancer Society and the American Heart Association. Some serve as commissioned officers in the medical service and hospitals of the various armed forces or work for the U.S. Public Health Service or the Department of Veterans Affairs.

Health services managers put in long hours. They are on call at all times for emergency situations that affect the functioning of the institutions. They have very heavy workloads and are constantly under a great deal of pressure. Traveling may also be a part of the job, attending meetings and inspecting satellite facilities.

Qualifications, Education, and Training   Health services managers should have health and vitality, maturity, sound judgment, tact, patience, the ability to motivate others, good communication skills, and sensitivity for people.

Good grades in high school are important. Courses should include English, science, mathematics, business, public speaking, and social studies. Volunteer work or a part-time job in a hospital is helpful.

Preparation for this career includes the completion of an academic program in health administration that leads to a bachelor's, master's, or Ph.D. degree. The various levels of degree programs offer different levels of career preparation. Most health care organizations prefer to hire administrators with at least a master's degree in health administration, hospital administration, public health, or business administration. Usually, larger organizations require more academic preparation for their administrative positions.

The administrators of nursing homes must be licensed. Licensing requirements vary from state to state, but all require a specific level of education and experience.

For clinical department heads, a degree in the appropriate field and work experience plus higher degrees may be necessary.

Potential and Advancement   Health Services Manager is a very broad term for a field that is constantly changing. With major changes in group practices and managed health care, health services managers will be in demand. In 1994, health services managers held 315,000 jobs. Significant

growth is projected for this field through the year 2005 as the increasing number of people 85 years old and over create a greater demand for health services.

The most opportunities will be in hospitals as well as in hospital subsidiaries that provide services such as ambulatory surgery, alcohol and drug abuse rehabilitation, hospice facilities, physicians' offices, outpatient care facilities, health and allied services, and nursing and long-term care facilities. Opportunities will be good in home health care and non-traditional health organizations such as managed care operations.

In spite of the tremendous growth in this field, there will be keen competition for upper-level management jobs in hospitals.

Health services managers advance as they move into higher-paying positions with more responsibilities. They also may advance by transferring to another health care facility or organization.

Income   The median salary for administrators in group practices was $65,000 in 1994. Salaries for the heads of clinical departments ranged from $55,000 to $88,000 in 1995. Nursing home administrators had a median annual compensation of $47,400 in 1994. Salaries vary depending on the manager's level of experience, education, and expertise, the type and size of health facility, the geographic location, and the type of ownership.

Additional Sources of Information

American College of Health Care Administrators
325 S. Patrick Street
Alexandria, VA 22314

American College of Healthcare Executives
One North Franklin Street, Suite 1700
Chicago, IL 60606

Association of University Programs in Health Administration
1911 North Fort Myer Drive, Suite 503
Arlington, VA 22209

Podiatrist

The Job   The diagnosis and treatment of diseases and deformities of the feet is the special field called podiatry. Podiatrists treat corns, bunions, calluses, ingrown toenails, skin and nail diseases, deformed toes, arch disabilities, ankle and foot injuries, heel spurs, and infections. If a person's feet show symptoms of medical disorders that affect other parts of the body (such as arthritis or diabetes), the podiatrist will refer the patient to a medical doctor while continuing to treat the patient's foot problem.

In the course of diagnosis, podiatrists may take x-rays and perform blood tests or other pathological tests. They perform surgery; fit corrective devices; and prescribe drugs, physical therapy, and proper shoes.

Most podiatrists provide all types of foot care, but some specialize in foot surgery, orthopedics (bone, muscle, and joint disorders), children's foot ailments, foot problems of the elderly, or public health. They also may subspecialize in areas such as sports medicine, dermatology, radiology, or diabetic foot care.

Some podiatrists purchase established practices or spend their early years in a salaried position while gaining experience and earning the money to set up their own practices. Podiatrists in full-time salaried positions usually work in hospitals, podiatric medical colleges, or for other podiatrists. Public health departments and the Department of Veterans Affairs also employ both full- and part-time podiatrists, and some serve as commissioned officers in the armed forces.

Places of Employment and Working Conditions   Podiatrists work in all sections of the country but are usually found in or near one of the seven states that have colleges of podiatric medicine, including California, Florida, Illinois, Iowa, New York, Pennsylvania, and Ohio.

Most podiatrists are in private practice, work about 40 hours a week, and set their own schedules. They also spend some hours handling the administration and paperwork of their practice, visiting nursing homes, and performing surgery. Podiatrists who work for hospitals or HMOs may be required to work nights or weekends. This is not physically strenuous work, a fact that allows practitioners in private practice to work past normal retirement age.

Qualifications, Education, and Training   Anyone interested in a career as a podiatrist should have scientific aptitude, manual dexterity, and an ability to work with people.

High school courses in mathematics and science are important preparation.

The degree of doctor of podiatric medicine (D.P.M.) is available after successful completion of at least three years of college and four years of a school of podiatric medicine. Competition for entry into these schools is strong and, although three years of college is the minimum requirement, most successful applicants have a bachelor's degree and an overall grade point average of B or better. College study must include courses in English, chemistry, biology or zoology, physics, and mathematics. All schools of podiatric medicine also require applicants to take the Medical College Admission Test (MCAT).

The first two years in podiatry school are spent in classroom and laboratory study of anatomy, bacteriology, chemistry, pathology, physiology, pharmacology, and other basic sciences. In the final two years, students obtain clinical experience. Additional study and experience are necessary for practice in a specialty. These residency programs last one to three years.

All podiatrists must be licensed. Requirements include graduation from an accredited college of podiatric medicine and passing grades on written and oral state board proficiency examinations. Many states also require a residency in a hospital or clinic. A majority of states grant licenses without examination to podiatrists licensed by another state.

There are a number of certifying boards for podiatric specialties. Certification means that the D.P.M. meets higher standards than those required for licensure.

Potential and Advancement   There are about 13,000 practicing podiatrists, most of them located in large cities. Employment in this field is expected to grow, and opportunities for graduates to establish new practices or enter salaried positions should be good through the year 2005.

Increasing population, especially the growing number of older people who need foot care and who are covered by Medicare, will contribute to the demand for podiatrists.

Income   Most newly licensed podiatrists set up their own practices and, as in new practices in most fields, earn a great deal less in the early years than they will after a few years in practice. The median net income of all podiatrists was $95,600 in 1994.

Additional Sources of Information

American Association of Colleges of Podiatric Medicine
1350 Piccard Drive, Suite 322
Rockville, MD 20850-4307

American Podiatric Medical Association
9312 Old Georgetown Road
Bethesda, MD 20814-1621

Prosthetist and Orthotist

The Job   Prosthetists work with patients who have lost limbs or partial limbs, and orthotists help patients who have disabled limbs or spines. Prosthetists construct replacement limbs, called prostheses. Orthotists design corrective devices, such as braces, called orthoses.

Prosthetists or orthotists receive a prescription from a physician for patients who have lost a limb or have a handicap. The prosthetist or orthotist then examines the patient and takes the necessary measurements to make sure that the device will fit properly. Each device is designed and constructed to meet a patient's individual needs.

The prosthetists and orthotists then make the device, using power and hand tools and leather, wood, or plastic. Once the device is completed, the prosthetist or orthotist fits it to the patient and makes any necessary adjustments or alterations. He or she then works with other members of the health care team, such as the physician or therapist, to help the patient adjust to the device.

Places of Employment and Working Conditions   Prosthetists and orthotists work in departments of prosthetics and orthotics in hospitals, clinics, and rehabilitation centers. Others have their own private practices.

Prosthetists and orthotists usually work in clean, well-lighted offices, examination rooms, and fitting rooms. Lab workers may sometimes have to cope with noise and fumes. Forty-hour, five-day workweeks are typical, with very little overtime work.

Qualifications, Education, and Training   Important qualities for workers in this field include patience, compassion, and creativity. Prosthetists and orthotists should have an aptitude for science and engineering.

A bachelor's degree in prosthetics or orthotics is necessary for work in this field. Course work includes biology, anatomy, physics, and engineering. There is a great deal of lab work, making and fitting devices.

While certification is not required, those who are certified have better opportunities available. The American Board for Certification in Orthotics and Prosthetics certifies those who have a bachelor's degree in prosthetics or orthotics from a board-approved college or university, at least one year of clinical experience, and a passing grade on an exam. Those who meet these qualifications are a certified prosthetist (C.P.), certified orthotist (C.O.), or certified prosthetist-orthotist (C.P.O.).

Potential and Advancement   Because of the growth of the elderly population, better access to medical and rehabilitation care brought about by expanding insurance coverage, and continuing advancement in this field, job opportunities should be good through the year 2005.

Prosthetists and orthotists may advance by becoming heads of departments. Others advance by starting their own private practice. Some become teachers or researchers.

Income   The average starting salary for prosthetists and orthotists is more than $20,000 a year. Those with experience earn between $24,000 and $30,000 a year. Practitioners with certification can earn even more; in hospitals salaries for certified workers range from $30,000 to $38,000.

Additional Sources of Information

American Academy of Orthotists and Prosthetists
717 Pendleton Street
Alexandria, VA 22314

American Board for Certification in Orthotics and Prosthetics
717 Pendleton Street
Alexandria, VA 22314

International Society for Prosthetics and Orthotics
U.S. National Member Society
317 East 34th Street
New York, NY 10016

Psychiatrist

The Job   A psychiatrist is a medical doctor (physician) who specializes in the problems of mental illness and emotional disorders. (See Allopathic Physician and Osteopathic Physician.) Because a psychiatrist is also a physician, he or she is licensed to use a wider variety of treatments—including drugs, hospitalization, somatic (shock) therapy—than others who provide treatment for the mentally ill. Approximately 11 percent of physicians specialize in psychiatry.

Psychiatrists may specialize as to psychiatric technique and age or type of patients treated, such as child or adolescent psychiatry. Others focus on the elderly, treating the problems of aging, senility, and depression.

Most psychiatrists are *psychotherapists* who treat individual patients directly. They sometimes treat patients in groups or in a family group.

Psychotheraphy is a technique of verbal therapy and may be supplemented with other treatments such as medication. Some psychiatrists are *psychoanalysts* who specialize in a technique of individual therapy based on the work of Sigmund Freud. Psychiatrists who practice this specialty must themselves undergo psychoanalysis in the course of their training. *Child psychiatrists* specialize in the treatment of children.

Some psychiatrists work exclusively in research, studying such things as the effect of drugs on the brain or the basic sciences of human behavior. Others teach at the college and university level. Research and teaching psychiatrists, however, usually combine their work with a certain amount of direct patient care.

In addition to private practice, psychiatrists work in clinics, general hospitals, and private and public psychiatric hospitals. The federal government employs a number of psychiatrists in the Veterans Administration and the U.S. Public Health Service.

Related jobs are psychologist and physician.

Places of Employment and Working Conditions   Psychiatrists work in all parts of the country, almost always in large metropolitan areas or near universities and medical schools.

This field can be emotionally wearing on the psychiatrist. The shortage of psychiatrists and the increasing demand for psychiatric services means that many practitioners are overworked and often cannot devote as much time as they would like to each individual patient.

The expense and time involved in securing an education for this field deters some people from pursuing psychiatry as a career.

Most psychiatrists have their own practices or practice in groups with other psychiatrists. Some work on staff at hospitals or mental health facilities.

Qualifications, Education, and Training   More than in any other field, the personality of the psychiatrist is very important. Emotional stability, patience, the ability to empathize with the patient, and a manner that encourages trust and confidence are absolutely necessary. The psychiatrist must be inquisitive, analytical, and flexible in the treatment of patients and must have great self-awareness of his or her own limitations and biases.

A high school student interested in this field should take a college preparatory course strong in science.

After high school, the training of a psychiatrist takes from 12 to 14 years. (Educational requirements for a physician are detailed under the job description for allopathic physician.)

After receiving an M.D. degree and completing a one-year medical internship in a hospital approved by the American Medical Association (AMA), a prospective psychiatrist begins a three- to four-year psychiatric specialty program. This program must take place in a hospital approved for this purpose by both the AMA and the American Psychiatric Association.

Training is carried on during a residency program that requires study, research, and clinical practice under the supervision of staff psychiatrists. After completion of the program and two years of experience, a psychiatrist is eligible to take the psychiatry examination of the American Board of Neurology and Psychiatry. Successful applicants then receive a diploma from this specialty board and are considered to be fully qualified psychiatrists.

At this point, a psychiatrist who wishes to specialize in child psychiatry must complete an additional two years of training, usually in a children's psychiatric hospital or clinic. A diploma in child psychiatry is then awarded after successful completion of the required examination.

Psychiatrists must also fulfill state licensing requirements before starting the residency period. Licensing requirements are explained in the job description for allopathic physician.

Potential and Advancement   Job opportunities are excellent for psychiatrists through the year 2005. Although there is currently an oversupply in some areas of the United States, some predict a shortage, especially in areas such as child psychiatry.

Psychiatrists may advance by building their practices. Some become experts in a certain field of psychiatry. Those employed in psychiatric hospitals may advance to administrative positions, and those who teach in colleges and universities may advance through the academic ranks to become full professors.

Income   During training, psychiatric residents receive a salary. Their average annual earnings are about $30,000. Experienced psychiatrists' earnings are similar to other physicians' earnings. Their average starting salary is about $85,000, with median net income in 1993 of $120,000.

Additional Sources of Information

American Medical Association
535 North Dearborn Street
Chicago, IL 60610

American Psychiatric Association
1400 K Street, NW
Washington, DC 20005

Psychologist

The Job   Psychologists study the behavior of individuals and groups to understand and explain their actions. Psychologists gather information through interviews and tests, by studying personal histories, and by conducting controlled experiments.

Psychologists may specialize in a wide variety of areas. *Experimental psychologists* study behavior processes by working with human beings as well as rats, monkeys, and pigeons. Their research includes motivation, learning and retention, sensory and perceptual processes, and genetic and neurological factors in human behavior. *Developmental psychologists* study the patterns and causes of behavior change in different age groups. *Personality psychologists* study human nature, individual differences, and the ways in which these differences develop.

Social psychologists examine people's interactions with others and with the social environment. Their studies include group behavior, leadership, and dependency relationships. *Environmental psychologists* study the influence of environments on people; *physiological psychologists* study the relationship of behavior to the biological functions of the body.

Psychologists often combine several of these or other specialty areas in their work. They further specialize in the setting in which they apply their knowledge.

Clinical psychologists constitute the largest specialty. They work in mental hospitals or clinics or maintain their own practices. They provide individual, family, and group psychotheraphy programs. They may collaborate with physicians and other specialists in developing and implementing treatment and intervention programs. Some work with medical and surgical patients in rehabilitation settings, or with the mentally and emotionally disturbed. *Counseling psychologists* help people with the problems of daily life—personal, social, educational, or vocational. *Educational psychologists* apply their expertise to problems in education while *school psychologists* work with students and diagnose educational problems, help in adjustment to school, and solve learning and social problems.

Others work as *industrial and organizational psychologists* (personnel work), *engineering psychologists* (human-machine systems), and *consumer psychologists* (what motivates consumers).

About 19,000 psychologists work in colleges and universities as teachers, researchers, administrators, or counselors. Most of the rest work in hospitals, clinics, rehabilitation centers, and other health facilities. The remainder work for federal, state, and local government agencies; correctional institutions; research firms; or in private practice.

Related jobs are psychiatrist, rehabilitation counselor, guidance counselor, marriage counselor, and social worker.

Places of Employment and Working Conditions

Psychologists work in communities of all sizes. The largest concentrations are in areas with colleges and universities.

Working hours for psychologists are flexible in general. Their specialties, however, determine their schedules. Clinical and counseling psychologists, for example, often work in the evening to accommodate the work and school schedules of their patients.

Clinical, school, and counseling psychologists in private practice have pleasant, comfortable offices. Those employed by hospitals, nursing homes, and other health facilities may work weekends, nights, and holidays. Some psychologists are employed as faculty by colleges, universities, and medical centers. Government agencies employ about one-sixth of all psychologists.

Qualifications, Education, and Training

Sensitivity to others and an interest in people are very important as are emotional stability, patience, and tact. Research requires an interest in detail, accuracy, and communication skills. Sensitivity, compassion, and the ability to lead and inspire others are especially important in counseling.

High school preparation should emphasize science and social science skills.

A bachelor's degree in psychology or a related field such as social work or education is only a first step, because a Ph.D. is the minimum requirement for employment as a psychologist. Those with only a bachelor's degree will be limited to jobs as research or administrative assistants in mental health centers, vocational rehabilitation offices and correctional programs, government, or business. Some may work as secondary school teachers if they complete state certification requirements.

Stiff competition for admission into graduate psychology programs means that only the most highly qualified applicants are accepted. College grades of B or higher are necessary.

At least one year of graduate study is necessary to earn a master's degree in psychology. Those with a master's degree qualify to work under the supervision of a psychologist and collect and analyze data and administer and interpret some kinds of psychological tests. They may also qualify for certain counseling positions such as school psychologists.

Three to five years of additional graduate work are required to earn a Ph.D. in psychology. Clinical and counseling psychologists need still another year or more of internship or other supervised experience. Some programs also require competence in a foreign language.

A dissertation based on original research that contributes to psychological knowledge is required of Ph.D. candidates. Another degree in this field is the Psy.D. (doctor of psychology). Acquisition of this degree is based on practical work and examinations rather than a dissertation. Over 600 universities offer either a master's or full Ph.D. program. Only a few schools offer the Psy.D.

The American Board of Professional Psychology awards diplomas in clinical, clinical neuropsychology, counseling, forensic, industrial and organizational, and school psychology. Candidates must have a Ph.D. or Psy.D. and five years of experience, pass an examination, and provide professional endorsements.

State licensing and certification requirements vary but usually require a Ph.D. or Psy.D., one to two years of professional experience, and a written examination.

Potential and Advancement   There are about 144,000 people working as psychologists. Employment in this field is expected to grow, but opportunities will be best for those with doctoral degrees.

Traditional academic specialties such as experimental, physiological, and comparative psychology will provide fewer job opportunities than the applied areas of school, clinical, counseling, health, industrial, and engineering psychology. However, the need to combat alcohol and drug abuse, marital strife, family violence, crime, and other problems currently plaguing society should stimulate the need for clinical psychologists.

Income   Median salaries for experienced psychologists with doctoral degrees are $42,100 in educational institutions; $40,000 in state and local governments and hospitals and clinics; $34,500 in nonprofit organizations; and $60,100 in business and industry. Some psychologists have much higher earnings, particularly those in private practice.

Additional Sources of Information

American Psychological Association
Educational Affairs Office
1200 17th Street, NW
Washington, DC 20036

American Psychological Association
Research Office and Education in Psychology and Accreditation Offices
750 1st Street, NE
Washington, DC 20002

National Association of School Psychologists
4030 East West Highway, Suite 402
Bethesda, MD 20814

Association of State and Provincial Psychology Boards
P.O. Box 4389
Montgomery, AL 36103-4389

Nursing

Registered Nurse
Licensed Practical Nurse
Nurse Practitioner
Nursing Aide
Home Health Aide

Nursing   The nursing field extends a number of opportunities to be a very important part of the health care team. Nursing involves direct patient contact, and varied skills and abilities. Often, a nurse is the first person a sick or troubled patient will see in a health care setting. A nurse has a unique opportunity to ensure that a patient's comforts and needs are cared for, and can make a difference in every patient's life. Careers in nursing are demanding, but extremely rewarding.

This section covers careers as a registered nurse, licensed practical nurse, nurse practitioner, nursing aide, and home health aide.

Registered Nurse

The Job   Registered nurses (RNs) play a major role in health care. As part of a health care team, they administer medications and treatments as prescribed by a physician, provide skilled bedside nursing care for the sick and the injured, and work toward the prevention of illness and the promotion of good health. They are typically concerned for the whole person, providing for the physical, mental, and emotional needs of patients.

Most nurses are employed in hospitals, where they usually work with a group of patients requiring similar care such as a postsurgery floor, the children's area (pediatrics), or the maternity section. Some specialize in operating room work.

Doctors, dentists, and oral surgeons employ nurses in their offices to perform routine laboratory and office work in addition to nursing duties. Industries employ nurses to assist with health examinations, treat minor injuries of employees, and arrange for further medical care if it is necessary. Industrial nurses may also do some recordkeeping and handle claims for medical insurance and workers' compensation.

Community health nurses work with patients in their homes, schools, public health clinics, and in other community settings. Nurses also teach in nursing schools and conduct continuing education courses for registered and licensed practical nurses.

Private duty nurses are self-employed nurses who provide individual care in hospitals or homes for one patient at a time when the patient needs constant attention. This care may be required for just a short time or for extended periods.

The federal government employs nurses in Veterans Administration hospitals and clinics, in the U.S. Public Health Service, and as commissioned officers in the armed forces.

Nursing was once considered a field for women, but this is rapidly changing and men are entering the field in increasing numbers in recent years.

Places of Employment and Working Conditions

Nurses are usually on their feet most of the day. Those who work in hospitals, nursing homes, or as private duty nurses must be prepared to work evenings, weekends, and holidays.

Most nurses work in pleasant, comfortable medical facilities. Home health and public health nurses travel to private homes, schools, community centers, and other sites. Because patients in hospitals and other facilities require 24-hour care, nurses may work nights, weekends, and holidays. Office nurses usually work regular business hours.

Qualifications, Education, and Training

Nurses need both physical and emotional stamina to cope with the stresses of their jobs. They face the dangers of infectious diseases (such as hepatitis and AIDS) and the hazards of working with radiation, chemicals, and gases. They also must be careful to avoid back injuries and muscle strains when moving patients. Nurses need the ability to follow orders precisely, use good judgment in emergencies, and cope with human suffering, and they must have good physical and emotional stamina. Nurses should be caring and sympathetic. They must be responsible and able to supervise others.

In high school, students should take a college preparation program with an emphasis on science.

There are three types of training for registered nurses. Many hospitals offer three-year diploma programs in their own nursing schools that combine classroom instruction and clinical experience within the hospital. Four-year bachelor's degree programs are available at many colleges (B.S.N.). Two-year associate degree programs are offered by some junior and community colleges (A.D.N.). These degree programs are combined with clinical practice in an affiliated hospital or health care facility. All students graduating from an accredited nursing school must pass a national licensing examination to obtain a nursing license.

A bachelor's degree is required for administrative or management positions in nursing; research, teaching, and clinical specializations usually require a master's degree. Individuals who are considering nursing as a career should carefully consider entering a B.S.N. program, since advancement opportunities are broader with this degree. Changes in licensure requirements may raise the educational requirements to a bachelor's degree.

Potential and Advancement   There were about 1,906,000 registered nurses, in 1994, one-fourth of them working part time. Future employment opportunities should be excellent for some time due to a current need for nurses. Nursing opportunities exist in every community; there are shortages of qualified nurses in many inner-city areas and in some southern states. Employment prospects for nurses with specialized training in fields such as intensive care, geriatrics, and oncology are excellent.

Experienced hospital nurses can advance to head nurse or assistant director or director of nursing services. Many supervisory and management positions require a bachelor's degree, however. Further advancement necessitates a master's degree. Nurses can advance to clinical nurse specialist, nurse practitioner, certified nurse-midwife, or nurse anesthetist through one or two years of graduate training.

Income   The median annual salary of staff nurses working a 40-hour week was $35,256 in 1994. For head nurses the median was $50,700; clinical nurse specialists, $47,674; and nurse anesthetists, $73,444.

Additional Sources of Information

American Nurses' Association
600 Maryland Ave. SW
Washington, DC 20024-2571

Communications Department
National League for Nursing
350 Hudson Street
New York, NY 10014

American Association of Colleges of Nursing
1 Dupont Circle, Suite 530
Washington, DC 20036

Licensed Practical Nurse

The Job   Licensed practical nurses (LPNs) provide much of the bedside care for patients in hospitals, nursing homes, and extended care facilities.

They work under the direction of physicians and registered nurses and perform duties that require technical knowledge but not the professional education and training of a registered nurse. In some areas such as Texas and California they are called licenses vocational nurses.

Most LPNs provide basic bedside care. They take and record temperatures and blood pressures, change dressings, administer certain prescribed medicine, bathe patients, care for newborn infants, give alcohol rubs and massages, apply ice packs and hot water bottles, and insert catheters.

Those who work in private homes provide daily nursing care and sometimes prepare meals for the patient as well. LPNs employed in physicians' offices or clinics may perform some clerical chores and handle appointments. In nursing homes, LPNs may also evaluate residents' needs, develop health care plans, and supervise nursing aides.

Places of Employment and Working Conditions   Licensed practical nurses work in all areas of the country, most of them in hospitals. Others work in nursing homes, clinics, physicians' offices, and private homes.

LPNs usually work a 40-hour week, but since patients require 24-hour care, they may work some nights, weekends, and holidays. They spend most of their working hours on their feet and help patients move in bed, stand, or walk. They also experience the stress of working with sick patients and their families.

LPNs face many hazards and difficulties on their jobs. They often come into contact with caustic chemicals, radiation, and infectious diseases. They may also suffer from back injuries and muscle strains when moving patients. The people they take care of may often be confused, angry, or depressed.

Qualifications, Education, and Training   Anyone interested in working as a practical nurse should have a caring and sympathetic nature, be emotionally stable, and have physical stamina. The ability to follow orders and work under close supervision is also necessary.

A high school diploma is usually necessary for enrollment in a training program. One-year, state-approved programs are offered by trade, technical, and vocational schools; high schools; junior colleges; local hospitals; health agencies; and private institutions. Some army training programs are also state approved.

Applicants for state licensing must complete a program in practical nursing that has been approved by the state board of nursing and must pass a written examination. In 1993, there were approximately 1,098 state-approved programs for practical nursing training.

Most practical nursing programs include both classroom study and supervised clinical practice, usually in a hospital setting.

Potential and Advancement   There are about 626,000 licensed practical nurses. The employment outlook for LPNs is very good through the next decade, due to a rapidly growing population of the elderly, increases in employment in nursing homes, and early release of patients from hospitals.

Advancement in this field is limited without formal education or additional training. Training programs in some hospitals help LPNs complete the educational requirements necessary to become registered nurses while they continue to work part time.

Income   Starting salaries for LPNs working in hospitals average about $19,000 a year. Experienced LPNs average between $23,000 and $28,000 a year. Median earnings in a nursing home in 1994 was $23,900.

Additional Sources of Information

Communications Department
National League for Nursing
350 Hudson Street
New York, NY 10014

National Association for Practical Nurse Education and Service, Inc.
1400 Spring Street, Suite 310
Silver Spring, MD 20910

National Federation of Licensed Practical Nurses, Inc.
P.O. Box 1088
Raleigh, NC 27619

American Health Care Association
1201 L Street, NW
Washington, DC 20005

Nurse Practitioner

The Job   A nurse practitioner is a registered nurse who has advanced education and clinical training in a health care specialty area. Specialty areas include family practice, pediatrics, acute care/emergency, geriatrics, and obstetrics/gynecology/midwifery. Nurse practitioners are health care providers who provide nursing and medical services to individuals, families, and groups. They diagnose and manage acute and chronic disease. Health promotion and disease prevention are major concerns of nurse practitioners. Services they provide include ordering, conducting, and interpreting appropriate diagnostic and laboratory tests, prescribing pharmacologic agents, and treatments of nonpharmacologic therapies. Teaching and counseling of individuals and families are also important responsibilities. Nurse practitioners are also permitted to perform some services, such as physical examinations, which have been traditionally handled only by physicians.

Places of Employment and Working Conditions   Nurse practitioners work in hospitals, public health clinics, and private physician offices. Some work in inner-city or rural clinics where a physician comes only once or twice a week. The nurse practitioner independently provides health care services after consulting with the supervising physician.

Nurse practitioners usually work a 40-hour week. But as is the case in most health care fields, nights, weekends, and holidays may be required.

Qualifications, Education, and Training   Nurse practitioners should be compassionate, but professional. They should enjoy working with people. Good physical health, emotional stability, and leadership qualities are also important. A registered nurse needs to possess a desire to increase knowledge, improve skills and abilities, and assume more responsibility in order to successfully complete the master's degree and post-master's training needed to become a nurse practitioner.

Admission to most nurse practitioner programs requires a bachelor's degree. To further specialize in a specific medical field, there are programs which require a master's degree for admission. Most states have laws concerning the qualifications and practice of nurse practitioners. Students are required to pass certifying examinations given by the state. Most nurse practitioners are nationally certified in their specialty area.

Potential and Advancement   The need for primary caregivers is rapidly increasing. The health service industry is expected to increase substantially through the year 2005. Nurse practitioners will be in demand to take over some of the traditional and routine tasks of the physician, and to assist physicians in more complex procedures.

Nurse practitioners can advance through additional specialty training programs. Gaining experience and more responsibility can increase a nurse practitioner's salary.

Income   The salary of a nurse practitioner can vary by experience and geographic location. The average starting salary can be as high as $34,000. Most salaries are in the range of $40,000 to $60,000.

Additional Sources of Information

American College of Nurse Practitioners
1090 Vermont Avenue, NW, #800
Washington, DC 20005

American Nurses Credentialing Center (ANCC)
600 Maryland Avenue, SW, Suite 100 West
Washington, DC 20024-2571

Nursing Aide

The Job   Nursing aides, also called nursing assistants or hospital attendants, provide care for patients in hospitals and in long-term care facilities such as nursing homes. Working under the supervision of registered and licensed practical nurses, they perform some of the more routine patient care duties.

Hospital nursing aides' tasks include taking patients' temperature, pulse, and blood pressure; helping patients in and out of bed; escorting them to operating and examining rooms; and feeding, dressing, and bathing them. They make beds, serve meals, and move supplies. Aides also observe patients' physical, mental, and emotional conditions.

Nursing aides in nursing homes have a great deal of contact with patients—far more than other members of the staff. They are the primary caregivers and perform many of the same tasks as hospital nursing aides.

Places of Employment and Working Conditions   Almost half of all nursing aides work in nursing homes, and others work in hospitals and state and county mental institutions. Some work in residential care facilities or in private homes.

Full-time nursing aides usually work 40 hours a week or less. Because patients need round-the-clock care, their work hours may include evenings, nights, weekends, and holidays.

This job is physically demanding and includes some unpleasant tasks. Workers spend a great deal of time on their feet and may have to move patients who are paralyzed or help them get in and out of bed, stand, and walk. Job duties include emptying bed pans, changing soiled bed linens, and caring for depressed or irritable patients.

Qualifications, Education, and Training   Nursing aides must want to help people; they need to be patient, understanding, emotionally stable, and dependable.

Most employers require neither a high school diploma nor prior work experience. Some hospitals require work experience, and some nursing homes require aides to complete 75 hours of mandatory training and pass a written exam within four months of employment. This is a good field for young people to gain exposure to health care occupations since many employers accept applicants who are 17 or 18 years old.

There are some training programs for nursing aides in high schools, vocational-technical centers, and some nursing homes and community colleges.

Potential and Advancement   There are about 1,265,000 nursing aides, and job prospects through the year 2005 are excellent. Because of the growing elderly population, nursing aides will find jobs primarily in the growing number of nursing homes. Also nursing aides will be needed to care for the growing number of people whose lives are saved due to advanced medical technology but who never fully recover.

There are very limited opportunities for advancement in this field. There may be job opportunities for nursing aides who take additional training in a health care occupation.

Income   Annual earnings for full-time nursing aides range from $11,600 to $22,000 or more, with the median earnings being about $14,612 in 1994.

Additional Sources of Information

American Health Care Association
1201 L Street, NW
Washington, DC 20005

American Hospital Association
Division of Nursing
840 North Lake Shore Drive
Chicago, Il 60611

Home Health Aide

The Job   Most home health aides work with elderly, disabled, or ill clients. They help them live in their own homes instead of in a health care facility. Some aides work in homes where a parent is incapacitated, and also care for small children. Occasionally, home aides may provide housekeeping services, but their main service is in personal care and emotional support for their clients.

"Hands on" care includes helping clients move from their beds, bathe, dress, and groom. They also check vital signs, help with prescribed exercises, assist with medication routines, change nonsterile dressings, use special equipment (such as hydraulic lifts or respirators), and give massages and alcohol rubs. Aides also keep records of services performed and of the client's progress and condition.

Places of Employment and Working Conditions   Most home health aides are employed by home health care agencies, visiting nurse associations, residential care facilities, community volunteer agencies, hospitals, public health and welfare departments, and temporary help firms. A few are self-employed, and set their own schedules, fees, and client appointments.

The home health care aide has a varied schedule. Some may go to one home for years, others may see five or six clients in a day. Each client has a different personality and a different lifestyle. Some homes may be pleasant, others may be depressing. A part of each working day may be spent traveling from one client's home to another.

Qualifications, Education, and Training   Home health aides must be in good health. They must like to help people and not mind hard work. Aides should also be responsible, compassionate, emotionally stable, and cheerful. Since they work in private homes, they need to be discreet, honest, and tactful.

Most training for home health aides is on-the-job. However, the federal government has enacted guidelines and requires home health aides to pass a competency test covering twelve areas. These are communication skills; observation, reporting, and documentation of patient status; reading and recording vital signs; basic infection control procedures; basic elements of body function; maintenance of a clean, safe, and healthy environment; recognition of and procedures for emergencies; the physical, emotional, and developmental characteristics of the patients served; personal hygiene; safe transfer techniques; normal range of motion; and basic nutrition.

Federal law suggests at least 75 hours of classroom instruction and practical training supervised by a registered nurse. The Foundation for Hospice and Home Care offers a National Homemaker–Home Health Aide certification.

Potential and Advancement   The field of home health care will be one of the fastest-growing occupations through the year 2005. It may more than double its number of workers. This increase is due to several factors. First of all, the number of elderly people is projected to rise substantially. Baby boomers will soon be reaching the age at which they are more likely to have heart attacks and strokes. Patients are being moved out of hospitals and nursing facilities as quickly as possible to contain costs. And more portable equipment is being developed. Health care workers are also realizing that treatment for chronically ill or disabled people is often far more effective in the familiar settings of home rather than the cold, sterile environment of a hospital.

Advancement in this field is limited. The more experienced a health aide is, the more responsibilities and duties he or she will take on. Further education is necessary for advancement into more detailed nursing care.

Income   Earnings for home health care workers vary considerably. In 1994, the average hourly wage was $4.90 to $6.86. More experienced workers

earned up to $8.11. Most employers give pay increases with experience and added responsibility.

Additional Source of Information

Foundation for Hospice and Home Care/National Certification Program
519 C Street, NE
Washington, DC 20002

Dentistry

Dentist
Dental Assistant
Dental Hygienist
Dental Laboratory Technician

Dentistry   Dentistry is concerned with a very important aspect of every person's general health: the entire oral cavity, including the teeth, gums, temperomandibular joint, and supporting structures of the teeth. Each person of the dental health team aids in the prevention of oral disease, helps in restoring teeth and supporting structures, educating the population about dental health problems, prevention, and care, and works to make a difference in each patient's life. A person's smile, speech, eating and sleeping habits can all be affected by his or her oral health.

Careers in dentistry include the dentist, dental hygienist, dental assistant, and dental laboratory technician.

Dentist

The Job   About nine out of ten dentists are general practitioners who provide many types of dental care. They examine teeth and mouth tissues to diagnose and treat any diseases or abnormalities of the teeth, gums, supporting bones, and surrounding tissues. They extract teeth, fill cavities, design and insert dentures and inlays, and perform surgery. They also take and examine x-rays, place protective sealants on children's teeth, administer anesthetics, write prescriptions for patients' needs, and replace missing teeth with partial dentures, full dentures, or bridgework. Dentists can also implant a tooth that has been "knocked out," in certain circumstances. The dentist, or someone on his or her staff, takes dental and medical histories, cleans teeth, and provides instructions on proper diet and cleanliness to preserve dental health.

About 10 percent of all dentists are specialists. The two largest fields are made up of *orthodontists*, who straighten teeth, and *oral surgeons*, who operate on the mouth and jaws. Other specialties are pediatric dentistry (dentistry for children), periodontics (treatment of the gums), prosthodontics (artificial teeth and dentures), endodontics (root canal therapy), oral pathology (diseases of the mouth), and public health dentistry.

Close to 2,000 civilian dentists are employed by the federal government. These dentists work in hospitals and clinics of the Veterans Administration or in the U.S. Public Health Service.

Places of Employment and Working Conditions   Almost 90 percent of dentists work in private practice, which includes a wide variety of work settings and payment systems. Most general practitioners work four or five days per week. Many are solo practitioners who own their own dental practice and oversee the administration of the office. These dentists may hire receptionists, dental assistants, dental hygienists, and dental laboratory technicians. Of the dentists who work outside private practice, half are researchers, teachers, or administrators in dental schools. Others work in hospitals and clinics. The federal government employs about 2,000 dentists, primarily in the hospitals and clinics of the Department of Veterans Affairs and the U.S. Public Health Service.

Qualifications, Education, and Training
Students interested in dentistry as a career should possess a high degree of manual dexterity and scientific ability and have good visual memory and excellent judgement of space and shape. Good interpersonal skills are highly needed.

High school courses should include biology, chemistry, health, and mathematics.

Dental education is very expensive because of the length of time required to earn a dental degree. From three to four years of predental college work in the sciences and humanities is required by dental schools with most successful applicants having a bachelor's or a master's degree. Since competition for admission is stiff, dental schools give considerable weight to the amount of predental education and to college grades. Schools also require personal interviews and recommendations as well as completion of the admission testing program (Dental Aptitude Test, or DAT) used by all dental schools. In addition, state-supported dental schools usually give preference to residents of the state.

Dental school training lasts four academic years after college. The first two years consist of classroom instruction and laboratory work in anatomy, microbiology, biochemistry, physiology, clinical sciences, and preclinical technique. The remaining two years of the training period is spent in actual treatment of patients, under the supervision of licensed dentists. Upon graduation, students are awarded the degree of Doctor of Dental Surgery (D.D.S.). A few schools award the Doctor of Dental Medicine degree (D.M.D.).

A license to practice is required by all states and the District of Columbia. Requirements include a degree from a dental school approved by the Commission on Dental Accreditation and written and practical examinations. A passing grade on the written examination given by the National Board of Dental Examiners is accepted by most states as fulfilling part of the licensing requirements; 20 states will grant a license without examination to dentists already licensed by another state.

In 17 states, dentists who wish to specialize must have two or three years of graduate training, and, in some cases, pass an additional state examination. In the remaining states, a licensed dentist may engage in general or specialized dentistry. In these states, the additional education is also necessary to specialize; however, specialists are regulated by the state dental profession rather than by state licensing.

Potential and Advancement   There are about 142,000 active dentists, 90 percent of them in private practice. The demand for dentists is expected to grow because of population growth, increased awareness of the necessity of dental health, and the expansion of prepaid dental insurance benefits to employees in many industries. Elderly people are more likely to maintain dentition throughout their lives. Despite water fluoridation, young people will continue to need preventive checkups.

Income   Dentists setting up a new practice can look forward to a few lean years in the beginning. As the practice grows, income will rise rapidly, with average yearly earnings around $97,000 for those in general practice.

A practice can usually be developed most quickly in small towns where there is less competition from established dentists. Over the long run, however, earnings of dentists in urban areas are higher than earnings in small towns. Specialists generally earn more than general practitioners, averaging about $32,500 a year.

Additional Sources of Information

American Association of Dental Schools
1625 Massachusetts Avenue, NW
Washington, DC 20036

American Dental Association
Council on Dental Education
211 East Chicago Avenue
Chicago, IL 60611

Division of Dentistry
Public Health Service
U.S. Department of Health and Human Services
9000 Rockville Pike
Bethesda, MD 20014

Dental Assistant

The Job   Dental assistants work with dentists and dental hygienists as they examine and treat patients. They are usually employed in private dental offices and often combine office duties, such as making appointments, maintaining patient records, and billing, with chairside assisting.

Dental assistants prepare instruments and materials for treatment procedures, process dental x-ray films, sterilize instruments, prepare plaster casts of teeth from impressions taken by the dentists, provide postoperative instruction, instruct patients in oral health care, and sometimes provide oral medications to teeth and gums, fit rubber isolation dams on individual teeth before treatment by the dentist, and order dental supplies and materials.

Dental assistants are also employed in dental schools, hospital dental departments, state and local public health departments, and private clinics. The federal government employs them in the Public Health Service, the Veterans Administration, and armed forces.

Most dental assistants are women. Opportunities for part-time work are numerous, making this a good field for people with family responsibilities.

Places of Employment and Working Conditions   Dental assistants are employed in communities of all sizes, with the most job opportunities in large metropolitan areas.

A 40-hour workweek is usual for full-time dental assistants, but this may include some evening and Saturday hours in most dental offices.

The majority of dental assistants work in private dental offices. Some may work in dental schools, dental laboratories, hospitals, and clinics.

Qualifications, Education, and Training   Neatness and the ability to help people relax are important personal qualities. Manual dexterity is also important.

High school courses in biology, chemistry, health, typing, and office practices are helpful.

Most dental assistants acquire their skills on the job. Office skills often provide entry into a dental office where a beginner handles appointments, acts as receptionist, and performs routine clerical and recordkeeping chores. Dental assisting skills are then acquired over a period of time.

An increasing number of dental assistants are acquiring their training in formal programs at junior and community colleges and vocational and technical schools. Most of these programs require one year or less to complete.

Two-year programs include some liberal arts courses and offer an associate's degree upon completion. Some private schools offer four- to six-month courses in dental assisting, but these are not accredited by the Commission on Dental Accreditation. Dental assistants who receive their training in the armed forces usually qualify for civilian jobs.

Graduates of accredited programs may receive professional recognition by completing an examination given by the Dental Assisting National Board. They are then designated as certified dental assistants.

Potential and Advancement   There are about 166,000 people working as dental assistants; one-third work part time. Job opportunities should be excellent for the future, especially for graduates of formal training programs.

Dental assistants in large dental offices or clinics are sometimes promoted to supervisory positions. Others teach in or administer dental assisting education programs.

Income   Salaries vary widely from community to community and depend on training and experience, job responsibilities and duties, and size of dental practice.

The average income for full-time dental assistants is about $267 a week.

Additional Sources of Information

American Dental Assistants Association
203 N. LaSalle Street, Suite 1320
Chicago, IL 60601-1225

Dental Assisting National Board, Inc.
216 East Ontario Street
Chicago, IL 60611

Commission on Dental Accreditation
American Dental Association
211 E. Chicago Avenue, Suite 1814
Chicago, IL 60611

Dental Hygienist

The Job   Dental hygienists are specialists in preventive dental care. They are involved in both clinical dental work and education with specific responsibilities governed by the state in which the hygienist is employed.

Working as part of a dental health team under the supervision of a dentist, a dental hygienist may clean and polish a patient's teeth, removing plaque deposits and stains at the same time; apply medication for the prevention of tooth decay; take and develop x-rays; make model impressions of teeth for study; take medical and dental histories and dental charting; and provide instruction for patient self-care, diet, and nutrition. In some states, pain control and restorative procedures may also be performed by dental hygienists. Other important duties include the placement of sealants or cavity-preventative agents such as fluorides, placement of temporary fillings and periodontal dressings, and smoothing and polishing silver amalgam restorations.

Places of Employment and Working Conditions   Dental hygienists work in communities of all sizes.

They usually work a 35- to 40-hour week; those employed by a dentist in private practice usually have some weekend and evening hours. Dental hygienists are required to stand for a good part of the working day. Many work part time or under 35 hours per week. Flexible scheduling is a distinctive feature of this job. Full, part-time, evening, and weekend hours are possible.

Certain health protection procedures are important for anyone working in this field. These include regular medical checkups and strict adherence to established procedures for disinfection and use of x-ray equipment.

Some dental hygienists work in school systems where they examine students' teeth, assist dentists in determining necessary dental treatment, and report their findings to parents. They give instruction in proper mouth care and develop classroom or assembly programs on oral health.

Most dental hygienists are employed in private dental offices; many are employed part time.

Other employers are public health agencies, industrial plants, clinics and hospitals, dental hygienist schools, the federal government, and the armed forces (those with a bachelor's degree are commissioned officers). A few dental hygienists are involved in research projects, office management, and nursing homes.

Qualifications, Education, and Training

Dental hygienists use a variety of interpersonal and clinical skills to meet the dental health care needs of many different people each day. An enjoyment of diverse population groups and the ability to put people at ease are strong assets. Hygienists work with adults, children, the elderly, and the disabled. A love of teaching is also important as they provide oral health instruction for preventing disease and maintaining good oral health to their patients, in primary and secondary schools, and in other settings. Other important attributes are enjoyment in working with the hands, helping people, and helping to prevent disease. Personal good health, cleanliness and neatness, and a nice smile are also very important.

High school courses in the sciences and mathematics are recommended for anyone interested in this field. Chemistry, biology, and health are especially helpful.

There are two pathways to becoming a dental hygienist. Students can receive their education through community colleges or through university and baccalaureate programs. Since requirements vary, prospective students, advisers, and counselors should contact the particular dental hygiene program of interest.

An associate's degree is offered at the community-college level. Sometimes a program may require a year of college. Two years of college are required for a baccalaureate program, with the additional two years of dental hygiene courses earning a bachelor of science or arts degree. Both programs offer courses in anatomy, physiology, chemistry, pharmacology, microbiology, nutrition, histology, gum diseases, radiology, dental materials, and clinical dental hygiene. Liberal arts courses are also required for a bachelor's degree. Ten universities offer a master's degree in dental hygiene or related fields. Most teaching and research careers will require advanced degrees.

Licensing is required for all dental hygienists. Almost all states require that hygienists be graduates of accredited dental hygiene education programs. Schools are accredited when they meet the standards for accreditation by the Commission on Dental Accreditation of the American Dental Association (ADA). There are approximately 215 accredited programs in the United States.

A candidate for licensure must obtain a passing score on the Dental Hygiene National Board Examination, which is a written comprehensive examination. A state authorized licensure examination tests the candidate's clinical dental hygiene skills and procedures. Upon receipt of their license, dental hygienists may use "R.D.H." after their names to signify recognition by the state that they are registered dental hygienists.

Potential and Advancement   There are approximately one hundred thousand active dental hygienists in the United States today. Employment of dental hygienists is expected to grow much faster than the average for all occupations through the end of the decade. Dental hygiene will continue to be in the top ten growth disciplines in the health care professions through the year 2005. Some areas of the country are reporting current shortages. This continued demand is due to the fact that as the population grows older, most people are now retaining their teeth for a lifetime. Increased participation in dental health care plans, more group practice by dentists, and new dental health programs for children will also add to the demand. Many opportunities exist in rural settings, and flexible hours and part-time work are available.

Income   The salary of a dental hygienist varies, depending upon the geographic location, the type of practice, and the responsibilities associated with the specific position. In 1993, the average wage of a full-time dental hygienist was $21.10 per hour. Many dental hygienists also receive benefit packages from their employers which may include health insurance, paid vacation and sick leave, dues for membership in professional organizations, and tuition assistance for continuing education.

Additional Sources of Information

Division of Dentistry
Public Health Service
U.S. Department of Health and Human Services
9000 Rockville Pike
Bethesda, MD 20014

American Dental Association
Dept. of Career Guidance
211 E. Chicago Avenue, Suite 1804
Chicago, IL 60611

Division of Professional Development
American Dental Hygienists' Association (ADHA)
444 North Michigan Avenue, Suite 3400
Chicago, IL 60611-3902

Commission on Dental Accreditation
American Dental Association
211 E. Chicago Avenue, Suite 1814
Chicago, IL 60611

Dental Laboratory Technician

The Job   Dental laboratory technicians are skilled craftsworkers who make dental prosthetics such as crowns, bridges, and dentures according to the specifications of dentists. Some specialized technicians make appliances for straightening teeth and treating speech impediments while others make and repair contoured metal frames and retainers for teeth used in removable partial dentures.

Dentists send their requests along with specifications for the item to be made and a mold of the patient's mouth. The technician pours plaster into the mold and lets it set, creating a model of the patient's mouth. After careful examinations and observations of the model, the technician makes a wax tooth or teeth. This wax model is used to cast the metal base of the prosthetic device.

After the cast is poured and the metal base is made, the technician applies porcelain in layers to duplicate the exact color and shape of the tooth. The porcelain is baked on in a kiln. Then the prosthesis is glazed to give it a lacquered finish. The goal of the technician is to recreate exactly the lost tooth or teeth.

In some laboratories, technicians are responsible for completing specific steps in this process while in others, technicians may be responsible for many steps.

Places of Employment and Working Conditions   Most dental laboratory technicians work in commercial dental laboratories which are small, privately owned businesses employing fewer than five workers. There are a few larger laboratories employing over fifty workers. Other technicians work in dentists' offices and hospitals that provide dental services.

Work areas are usually clean and well lighted. Although this is generally not a strenuous job, there may be some pressure to meet deadlines. Workweeks are usually 40 hours.

Qualifications, Education, and Training   Dental laboratory technicians must be very precise and detail oriented. They must have good vision and a high degree of manual dexterity. The ability to follow directions is important.

Most dental laboratory technicians learn this craft on the job by performing basic tasks and then progressing to more complicated tasks. It usually takes three to four years to be fully trained.

There are formal programs that offer training in community and junior colleges, vocational-technical institutes, trade schools, high school vocational education programs, apprenticeships, and the armed forces. While the length of these programs and the extent of training vary, it typically takes two years to complete an accredited program. Usually an associate's degree or certificate or diploma are granted upon completion.

There are nearly 60 programs in dental laboratory technology accredited by the Commission on Dental Accreditation in conjunction with the American Dental Association.

Potential and Advancement   There are about 51,000 persons working as dental laboratory technicians.

This field will have a slower-than-average growth rate during the next decade. The large growth of the aging population will create some jobs for technicians, but a growing awareness of preventive dental health care and fluoridation of drinking water will result in greater dental health and reduce the need for dental prosthetic devices.

Successful technicians may advance by establishing laboratories of their own.

Income   Dental laboratory technicians working full time earned an average of $22,269 in 1993. Education, experience, and specialized skills usually bring higher pay.

Additional Sources of Information

Commission on Dental Accreditation
American Dental Association
211 East Chicago Avenue
Chicago, IL 60611

National Association of Dental Laboratories
3801 Mt. Vernon Avenue
Alexandria, VA 22305

Allied Health

Cytotechnologist (Histotechnologist)

Dietician

Electrocardiograph (EKG) Technician

Electroencephalograph (EEG) Technologist

Emergency Medical Technician (Paramedic)

Medical Laboratory Technologist

Nuclear Medicine Technologist

Occupational Therapist

Pharmacist

Physical Therapist

Physical Therapy Assistant

Radiologic (X-Ray) Technologist

Recreational Therapist

Rehabilitation Counselor

Respiratory Therapist

Social Worker

Speech Pathologist and Audiologist

Surgical Technologist

Allied Health   Careers in allied health are extremely varied, involving many different aspects of health care, any of which can be very satisfying. Each career has an important role in the entire network of health care. Each career involves its own set of skills, techniques, and educational requirements. Allied health careers are dynamic, as they are constantly changing with advances in medicine. New careers are also being added to the framework of allied health, as new medical procedures are developed, and medical research provides new techniques and machines to help overcome disease and increase patient comforts and needs.

Careers described in this section include cytotechnologist, dietician, electrocardiographer, electroencephalographer, emergency medicine technician, medical laboratory technologist, nuclear medicine technologist, occupational therapist, pharmacist, physical therapist and assistant, radiologic technologist, recreational therapist, rehabilitation counselor, respiratory therapist, social worker, speech pathologist, and surgical technician.

Cytotechnologist

The Job   Clinical laboratory testing is crucial to the detection, diagnosis, and treatment of disease. Cytotechnologists are specialized medical technologists who assist physicians by performing laboratory tests to determine body cell abnormalities. An abnormality in a body cell may indicate cancer, and the cytotechnologist's detection of a malignancy may mean the difference between life and death for a patient.

After receiving a physician's order for laboratory tests, the cytotechnologist prepares slides of body cells and microscopically examines them to determine whether there are any cell abnormalities. He or she then interprets the results of the tests and sends them back to the physician. The physician uses the test results to inform the patient of the absence or presence of a disease and to decide what course of treatment will be most effective.

Most cytotechnologists work in hospitals, but others work in independent laboratories, physicians' offices, clinics, health maintenance organizations (HMOs), public health agencies, pharmaceutical firms, and research institutions.

Places of Employment and Working Conditions   Cytotechnologists are in demand in all areas of the country, with the largest concentration of jobs in metropolitan areas.

Cytoftechnologists work in clean, well-lighted laboratories. Sometimes they must work with infectious specimens from patients with contagious diseases such as AIDS that have to be handled with great care. Odors are sometimes present in the laboratory, and workers must cope with the stress of performing their job both quickly and accurately.

Cytotechnologists who work in hospitals or laboratories that operate 24 hours a day may have to work day, evening, or night shifts. Weekend and holiday work is usually required since laboratories operate 365 days a year.

Qualifications, Education, and Training

A cytotechnologist, technically, is different from a *histotechnologist* ("cyto" means cell, and "histo" refers to tissues), but the two terms are often used interchangeably in the lay community. In any case, anyone interested in becoming either a cytotechnologist or a histotechnologist must be accurate and dependable and must have the ability to form analytical judgments based on the tests they perform and to cope with pressure. They must be detail-oriented and have problem-solving capabilities. Good interpersonal communication skills are also important.

A bachelor's degree with a major in medical technology or the life sciences and specialized training in cytotechnology is necessary for entry-level jobs. This educational training is offered in colleges, universities, and hospitals. Those who are interested in this career field should make sure that the program they are taking is accredited by the Committee on Allied Health Education and Accreditation (CAHEA) in cooperation with the National Accrediting Agency for Clinical Laboratory Sciences (NAACLS). They also should be aware that some states require workers to be licensed or registered.

Potential and Advancement

The field of cytotechnology offers excellent job prospects. There is currently a shortage of workers in this field, and the number of cytotechnology students is on the decline. Cytotechnologists are in demand, and the supply is currently not sufficient.

With graduate education, cytotechnologists may advance in several ways. They may be promoted to supervisory positions in large hospitals and laboratories. Other workers move on to employment with manufacturers of home diagnostic testing kits and laboratory equipment and supplies. Growth in independent medical laboratories and rapid growth in offices and clinics of physicians may also lead to increased employment of cytotechnologists.

Income

Median annual earnings of cytotechnologists were $37,107 in 1994. Annual salaries ranged from $29,772 to $43,477.

Additional Sources of Information

American Society for Medical Technology
2021 L Street, NW
Washington, DC 20036

American Medical Technologists
710 Higgins Road
Park Ridge, IL 60068

American Society of Cytology
1015 Chestnut Street, Suite 1518
Philadelphia, PA 19107

Committee on Allied Health and Accreditation
535 North Dearborn Street
Chicago, IL 60610

National Accrediting Agency for Clinical Laboratory Sciences
8410 W. Bryn Mawr Avenue, Suite 670
Chicago, IL 60631

Dietician

The Job   Dieticians plan nutritious and appetizing meals, supervise the preparation and service of food, and manage the purchasing and accounting for their department. Others are involved in research and education.

More than half of all dieticians are employed in hospitals, nursing homes, and other health care facilities. Colleges, universities, school systems, restaurants and cafeterias, large companies that provide food service for their employees, and food processors and manufacturers also employ dieticians.

Some serve as commissioned officers in the armed forces. The federal government also employs dieticians in Veterans Administration hospitals and in the U.S. Public Health Service.

Clinical dieticians form the largest group of dieticians. They plan the diets and supervise the service of meals to meet the nutritional needs of patients in hospitals, nursing homes, and clinics. They confer with doctors and instruct patients and their families on diet requirements and food preparation.

Management dieticians are responsible for large-scale meal planning and preparation. They purchase food, equipment, and supplies; enforce safety and sanitary regulations; and train and direct food service and supervisory workers. If they are directors of a dietetic department, they may also have budgeting responsibilities, coordinate dietetic service activities with other departments, and set department policy. In a small institution, the duties of administrative and clinical dieticians are usually combined into one position.

Research dieticians evaluate the dietary requirements of specific groups such as the elderly, space travelers, or those with a chronic disease. They also do research in food management and service systems and equipment. *Dietetic educators* teach in medical, dental, and nursing schools.

Nutritionists provide counseling in proper nutrition practices. They work in food industries, educational and health facilities, agricultural agencies, welfare agencies, and community health programs.

Places of Employment and Working Conditions

Dieticians are employed throughout the country with most job opportunities in large metropolitan areas and in areas with large colleges and universities.

Most dieticians work a 40-hour week, but this usually includes some weekend hours. There are many part-time opportunities for dieticians.

Over half of all dieticians work in hospitals and nursing homes. Some work in social service agencies, residential care facilities, diet workshops, physical fitness facilities, school systems, and the federal government. A few are self-employed and act as consultants to health care facilities and wellness programs, and see individual clients.

Qualifications, Education, and Training

Anyone interested in this career field should have scientific aptitude, organizational and administrative ability, and the ability to work well with people.

High school courses should include biology, chemistry, home economics, mathematics, and some business courses, if possible.

A bachelor's degree in the home economics department with a major in foods and nutrition or institutional management is the basic requirement for a dietician. Almost 260 schools offer undergraduate programs in the field.

A 9- to 12-month internship or a preprofessional practice program should also be completed by any dietician who wants professional recognition. These programs consist primarily of clinical experience under the direction of a qualified dietician. Some colleges and universities have coordinated undergraduate programs that enable students to complete both the clinical and bachelor's degree requirements in four years.

Vocational and technical schools as well as junior colleges also offer training in dietetic services. Students who complete these training courses can work as dietetic assistants or technicians and usually find ample job opportunities.

The American Dietetic Association registers dieticians who meet their established qualifications. The designation RD (registered dietician) is an acknowledgment of a dietician's competence and professional status.

Potential and Advancement   About 53,000 people worked as dieticians in 1994. Job opportunities, both full and part time, should be plentiful through the year 2005. There is an increased emphasis on the prevention of diseases through better nutrition and health habits.

Dieticians usually advance by moving to larger institutions. In a large institution, they may advance to director of the dietetic department. Some advance by entering some area of clinical specialization. Others become consultants or opt for careers in business and management. Advancement in research and teaching positions usually requires a graduate degree.

Income   Beginners in this field with five years or less experience earned a median annual salary of about $29,600 a year in 1993. Those with six to ten years of experience earned about $34,400 annually and those with twenty years of experience earned about $41,600 annually.

Additional Source of Information

The American Dietetic Association
216 West Jackson Boulevard, Suite 800
Chicago, IL 60606-6995

Electrocardiograph (EKG) Technician

The Job   By using a machine called an electrocardiograph, EKG technicians record tracings of heartbeats that show the electrical impulses given off by the heart muscle during and between heartbeats. This test is ordered by doctors to determine whether a patient has heart disease; to check the effectiveness of drugs used in treatment; and to study the changes in a patient's heart over a period of time.

The EKG technician attaches electrodes to a patient's chest, arms, and legs and applies a gel between the electrode and the patient's skin so the electrical impulses can be recorded. A stylus or inkpen records the heart's electrical impulses on graph paper as the technician operates different switches on the electrocardiograph and positions electrodes across the patient's chest.

After the technician has performed the test, he or she must prepare it for the physician's use. Technicians working with the most advanced EKG equipment must enter information into a computer for an analysis of the tracing. They must be able to detect errors in the tracings and provide the physician with an accurate reading. They must also point out any abnormalities in the tracings to the physician.

More experienced technicians may perform specialized tests, such as ambulatory monitoring, in which the patient wears a portable EKG (also known as a Holter monitor) while performing normal activities for a period of 24 to 48 hours, or stress testing, in which the patient is tested while walking on a treadmill.

Places of Employment and Working Conditions   EKG technicians work in physicians' offices, cardiac rehabilitation centers, HMOs, and clinics; most work in hospital cardiology departments. While they are employed throughout the country, most job opportunities are in large metropolitan areas.

EKG technicians usually work a 40-hour week, which may include weekend and holiday hours. Those working in hospitals may work evening hours. They spend a great deal of time walking and standing.

Qualifications, Education, and Training   EKG technicians must feel comfortable working with both machines and people. They must be able to follow instructions and cope well in an emergency situation.

EKG technicians must have a high school diploma. Courses in health, biology, and typing will help them in this occupation.

Most EKG technicians receive on-the-job training from an EKG supervisor or cardiologist. Training to perform a basic resting EKG takes 8 to 16 weeks. After four to five months, technicians have been trained to administer tests to critically ill patients, interpret graphs, and write reports for physicians. Four more months of training are necessary in order to perform more complicated tests.

One-year certification programs teach basic EKG testing, holter monitoring, and stress testing. Cardiovascular technologists are required to complete a two-year community college program. This includes one year of basic science and core courses, and one year of specialized laboratory instruction. These technologists perform more difficult tasks involving cardiac catheterization procedures.

Potential and Advancement
Cardiovascular technologists held about 30,000 jobs in 1994. EKG technicians held about 18,000 of those jobs. The field is expected to grow very slowly through the year 2005. Improved technology and computerization have increased productivity and decreased demand. Also, many hospitals are cutting back on personnel by training other staff members to perform EKG testing.

Technicians may advance by gaining experience and becoming supervisors, administrators, or managers. Others may transfer to jobs in equipment sales and marketing.

Income
EKG technicians in hospitals, medical schools, and medical centers earn average starting salaries of about $15,793 a year. Those who are more experienced and perform more complicated tests earn more than those who perform basic ones. Some technicians with more experience earn a median salary of $22,985 a year.

The average salary for the more highly trained cardiovascular technologist was about $32,000 in 1984.

Additional Sources of Information

National Society of Cardiovascular Technology/National Society of
    Pulmonary Technology (NSCT/NSPT)
1133 15th Street, NW, Suite 1000
Washington, DC 20005

American Society for Cardiovascular Professionals
10500 Wakeman Drive
Fredericksburg, VA 22407

Division of Allied Health Education and Accreditation, American Medical
    Association
515 N. State Street
Chicago, IL 60610

Electroencephalograph (EEG) Technologist

The Job   EEG technologists operate an important medical diagnostic machine, the electroencephalograph. Electroencephalographs measure the electrical activity of the human brain, and encephalograms (EEGs), the records produced, are used for several different purposes. Neurologists use them to determine the extent of brain injuries, the effects of infectious brain diseases, and whether the cause of a patient's mental or behavioral problems is organic. Surgeons use EEGs to monitor a patient's condition during surgery, and EEGs are also used to determine whether a patient is clinically dead. Physicians are able to give a better prognosis of a comatose patient's chances for recovery after analyzing an EEG.

EEGs are performed while patients are either resting or ambulatory. Technologists take a medical history from a patient and then attach electrodes to the patient's head and body. After making sure that the equipment is working properly, technologists select the correct instrument controls and electrodes that will produce the type of record the physician has ordered. They must be aware of any readings that come from somewhere other than the brain, such as eye movement or interference from other electrical sources, and correct them. They then analyze the test and select sections for the physician to examine. They must know the difference between normal and abnormal brain waves.

Sometimes EEG technologists have supervisory or administrative responsibilities. They also may have to perform EKGs or other procedures.

Places of Employment and Working Conditions   Most EEG technologists work in hospitals, but some work in neurology laboratories, neurologists' and neurosurgeons' offices, group medical practices, HMOs, urgent care centers and clinics, and psychiatric facilities.

EEG technologists work in a clean, well-lighted atmosphere. The job can be physically demanding; they spend a great deal of time on their feet and are required to do a lot of bending in working with very ill patients.

Technologists usually have a 5-day, 40-hour workweek with some overtime, but some may have to be on call during evening, weekend, and holiday hours.

Qualifications, Education, and Training   EEG technologists must have an aptitude for working with both humans and machinery. They should

have manual dexterity, good vision, and writing skills. They must be able to follow directions.

Technologists usually receive their training on the job; a high school diploma is necessary. Some hospitals, medical centers, community colleges, and vocational-technical schools offer one- or two-year formal training programs. Formal training with an associate degree or certificate is becoming more and more important. Fourteen programs have been accredited by the Joint Review Committee for the Accreditation of EEG Technology Training Programs. Graduates of these programs receive associate's degrees or certificates. These programs generally take from one to two years to complete and consist of laboratory experience plus classroom instruction in subjects such as human anatomy and physiology, neuroanatomy, neurophysiology, computer technology, and electronics.

Potential Advancement   There are about 6,400 EEG technologists, and this field is expected to grow rapidly through the year 2005. Greater acceptance of the value of the EEG and the willingness of health insurers to pay for this type of test will contribute to this growth. Opportunities for those with training in EEG technology should be excellent. Most growth will occur in private offices and clinics.

EEG technologists in hospital settings may advance by becoming chief EEG technologists, taking on more management and training responsibilities.

Income   EEG technologists have average annual starting salaries of $15,924. More experienced technologists earn yearly salaries up to $27,360. Those in supervisory or training positions usually command higher salaries. In 1994, the median annual salary was $24,710. Average maximum salary was $29,691.

Additional Sources of Information

Executive Office
American Society of Electroneurodiagnostic Technologists Inc.
204 W. Seventh
Carroll, IA 51401

Joint Review Committee on Electroneurodiagnostic Technology
Route 1
Box 63 A
Genoa, WI 54632

Emergency Medical Technician

The Job   Emergency medical technicians, or EMTs, are usually the first caregivers to arrive on the scene of a medical emergency. Their ability to provide medical care quickly and accurately may save a victim's life.

Upon arrival at the scene, EMTs must assess the situation and decide which emergency services must be given first. They must determine the victim's condition as well as whether he or she has any preexisting medical conditions, such as epilepsy or diabetes, that will affect the type of treatment given. Some of the medical treatments EMTs are trained to give include opening airways, restoring breathing, controlling breathing, treatment for shock, administering oxygen, assisting in childbirth, treating and resuscitating heart attack victims, and giving initial care to poison and burn victims.

Sometimes when a situation is very serious, EMTs must report directly to the hospital by radio, transmitting vital signs and other information, so that the hospital can then provide instructions for treatment.

Another difficulty EMTs sometimes face is that they must free trapped victims, as in a car accident or a collapsed building. They must somehow free the victim while making sure that he or she is not injured further.

If victims must be transported to the hospital, EMTs put them on stretchers, carry them to the ambulance, and place them inside, making sure that the stretcher is secure. One EMT drives the ambulance while the other stays with the victim and continues medical treatment. After the ambulance arrives at the hospital, the EMTs help get the victim into the emergency room and inform the physicians and nurses of their observations and the treatment they have given.

It is also the EMTs' responsibility to make sure that the ambulance is properly equipped and maintained. They must see that any supplies that have been used are either replaced or cleaned and sterilized and check the equipment to ensure that it is working properly. They also must see that the ambulance is in good working condition.

There are three classifications for EMTs: EMT-ambulance (EMT-A), EMT-intermediate, and EMT-paramedic. EMT-As are basic EMTs. EMT-intermediates and EMT-paramedics have received more training and are capable of giving additional types of medical treatment. They can administer intravenous fluids, administer drugs, interpret EKGs, perform endotracheal intubations, and use monitors and other complex equipment. A fourth level—EMT-defibrillator (EMT-D)—is emerging. These EMTs are trained in using electrical defibrillation to resuscitate heart attack victims.

Places of Employment and Working Conditions

EMTs are employed by private ambulance services; hospitals; and municipal police, fire, and rescue squad departments.

EMTs work inside and outside, sometimes in poor weather conditions. EMTs' services are needed 24 hours a day, so they are often required to work evenings, weekends, and holidays. This job is physically strenuous—it involves a great deal of lifting. There is also much pressure in this field— EMTs must make life-and-death decisions as part of their regular job.

Qualifications, Education, and Training

EMTs must be physically strong and healthy. They must be able to make good decisions quickly in stressful situations. They should be emotionally stable and have leadership abilities. EMTs should have a neat and clean appearance and a pleasant personality.

EMTs are required to undergo instruction in emergency medical care techniques. The U.S. Department of Transportation has designed a national standard training program. The course is 100 to 120 hours of classroom work plus 10 hours of internship. It is offered in all 50 states, the District of Columbia, and the Virgin Islands. The course is offered by police, fire, and health departments; hospitals; and medical schools, colleges, and universities.

Those taking the course learn how to deal with emergencies such as bleeding, fractures, oxygen administration, airway obstruction, cardiac arrest, and emergency childbirth.

After completing this course, students may take a two-day course in removing trapped victims and a five-day course in driving emergency vehicles.

To become an EMT-intermediate, EMT-As must take additional courses in patient assessment and the use of esophageal airways, intravenous fluids, and antishock garments. EMT-paramedics must complete between 750 and 2,000 additional hours of instruction.

Applicants to EMT training courses must be at least 18 years old, and have a high school diploma or its equivalent and a valid drivers license.

The National Registry of Emergency Medical Technicians registers EMT-paramedics who meet its standards. While registration is not a requirement, it does give greater credibility to EMTs who have earned it.

All 50 states have certification procedures. To maintain certification, all EMTs must register every two years. This requires an EMT to be currently working and to meet the continuing education requirement.

Potential Advancement   There were 138,000 EMTs in 1994. There will be some growth in employment through the year 2005. The rapid growth in the number of senior citizens and developments in the field of emergency medicine will create a demand for EMTs. However, the high cost of training and equipping EMTs may lessen opportunities. The best job prospects will be with municipal governments and private ambulance services.

EMTs who have advanced through the ranks to become EMT-paramedics must leave fieldwork to advance any further. They may become field supervisor, operations supervisor, operations manager, administrative director, and then executive director.

Another advancement route for EMTs is to become an instructor, but this usually requires a bachelor's degree in education.

Other EMTs leave the field altogether, becoming sales representatives for emergency medical equipment manufacturers. Other become police officers or firefighters. By getting more education, some are able to move into clinical or management careers in health or related fields.

Income   Earnings for EMTs depend on the level of their experience and training, the type of employer they have, and their geographical area.

Average starting salaries for EMT-As were $19,919 a year in 1995; for EMT-intermediates, $21,818; and EMT-paramedics, $23,861. The highest salaries are paid to EMTs working in fire departments.

Additional Sources of Information

National Association of Emergency Medical Technicians
102 W. Leake Street
Clinton, MS 39056

National Registry of Emergency Medical Technicians
P.O. Box 29233
Columbus, OH 43229

Medical Laboratory Technologist

The Job   Medical laboratory work often appeals to people who would like to work in the medical field but who are not necessarily interested in direct care of patients. Those who work in medical laboratories are involved in the analysis of blood, tissue samples, and body fluids. They use precision instruments, equipment, chemicals, and other materials to detect and diagnose diseases. In some instances, such as blood tests, they also gather the specimens to be analyzed.

The work of medical laboratory technologists is done under the direction of a pathologist (a physician who specializes in the causes and nature of disease) or other physician or scientist who specializes in clinical chemistry, microbiology, or other biological sciences.

Medical technologists, who have four or five years of training, usually perform a wide variety of tests in small laboratories; those in large laboratories usually specialize in a single area such as parasitology, blood banking, or hematology (study of blood cells). Some do research, develop laboratory techniques, or perform supervisory and administrative duties.

Medical laboratory technicians, who have two years of training, have much the same testing duties but do not have the in-depth knowledge of the technologists. Technicians may also specialize in a particular field but are not usually involved in administrative work.

Medical laboratory assistants have about one year of formal training. They assist the technologists and technicians in some routine tests and are generally responsible for the care and sterilization of laboratory equipment, including glassware and instruments, and do some recordkeeping.

Most technologies, technicians, and laboratory assistants work in hospital laboratories. Others work in physicians' offices, independent laboratories, blood banks, public health agencies and clinics, pharmaceutical firms, and research institutions. The federal government employs them in the U.S. Public Health Service, the armed forces, and the Department of Veterans Affairs.

Places of Employment and Working Conditions   Work in this field is available in all areas of the country, with the largest concentrations in the larger cities.

Medical laboratory personnel work a 40-hour week with night and weekend shifts if they are employed in a hospital. Laboratories are usually clean and well lighted and contain a variety of testing equipment and materials. Although unpleasant odors are sometimes present and the work involves the processing of specimens of many kinds of diseased tissue, few hazards exist because of careful attention to safety and sterilization procedures.

Qualifications, Education, and Training

A strong interest in science and the medical field is essential. Manual dexterity, good eyesight, and normal color vision are necessary. One must also show attention to detail and accuracy and have the ability to work under pressure and the desire to take responsibility for his or her own work.

High school students interested in this field should take courses in science and mathematics and should select a training program carefully.

Medical technologists must have a college degree and complete a specialized program in medical technology. This specialized training is offered by hospitals and schools in programs accredited by either the Committee on Allied Health and Accreditation (CAHEA) in cooperation with the National Accrediting Agency for Clinical Laboratory Sciences (NAACLS) or the Accrediting Bureau of Health Education Schools (ABHES). The programs are usually affiliated with a college or university. A few training programs require a bachelor's degree for entry; others require only three years of college and award a bachelor's degree at the completion of the training program. Those who wish to specialize must complete an additional 12 months of study with extensive lab work.

Advanced degrees in this field are offered by many universities and are a plus for anyone interested in teaching, research, or administration.

Technicians may receive training in two-year educational programs in junior colleges, in two-year courses at four-year colleges and universities, in vocational and technical schools, or in the armed forces.

Medical laboratory assistants usually receive on-the-job training. Some hospitals—and junior colleges and vocational schools in conjunction with a hospital—also conduct one-year training programs, some of which are accredited by the ABHES. A high school diploma or equivalency diploma is necessary.

Medical technologists may be certified by the Board of Registry of the American Society of Clinical Pathologists, the American Medical Technologists, the National Certification Agency for Medical Laboratory Personnel, or the Credentialing Commission of the International Society of Clinical Laboratory Technology. These same organizations also certify technicians.

Some states require technologists and technicians to be licensed. This usually takes the forms of a written examination. Other states often require registration.

Potential and Advancement   There are about 274,000 persons employed as medical laboratory workers. Medical laboratory technology is a good job opportunity field since, like the entire medical field, it is expected to grow steadily due to population growth and the increase in prepaid medical insurance programs. Job opportunities will probably be slightly better for technicians and assistants, because the increasing use of automated lab equipment will allow them to perform tests that previously required technologists. Technologists will be needed for supervisory and administrative positions, however, and will continue to be in demand in laboratories where their level of training is required by state regulations or employer preference. Fastest growth will occur in independent medical laboratories and physicians' offices and clinics.

Advancement depends on education and experience. Assistants can advance to the position of technician or technologist by completing the required education; technicians can advance to supervisory positions or complete the required education for technologists. Advancement to administrative positions is usually limited to technologists.

Income   Salaries in this field vary depending on employer and geographic location; the highest salaries are paid in the larger cities.

Newly graduated medical technologists start at about $26,033 a year; technicians at about $20,443. Experienced medical technologists earn an average of about $32,282 a year.

Additional Sources of Information

Accrediting Bureau of Health Education Schools
Oak Manor Office
29089 U.S. 20 West
Elkhart, IN 46514

American Medical Technologists
710 Higgins Road
Park Ridge, IL 60068

American Society of Clinical Pathologists
Board of Registry
P.O. Box 12270
Chicago, IL 60612

American Society for Medical Technology
2021 L Street, NW
Washington, DC 20036

International Society for Clinical Laboratory Technology
818 Olive Street
St. Louis, MO 63101

Nuclear Medicine Technologist

The Job   In nuclear medicine, radiation is used in the diagnosis and treatment of disease. Radiation, in the form of drugs called radiopharmaceuticals, is injected into patients or taken orally and is traced from outside the body to the organs or tissues where it settles in order to determine any of their abnormalities. Nuclear medicine technologists are the specially trained workers who perform these tests under the direction of a physician. They also explain testing procedures to patients.

Nuclear medicine technologists must prepare the correct dosage of the radiopharmaceutical and administer it to the patient orally, by injection, or by other means. They must be careful in preparing the radiopharmaceutical to keep the radiation dose to workers and the patient as low as possible.

Once the radiopharmaceutical has entered the patient's system, the technologist uses diagnostic imaging equipment to trace and photograph the radiopharmaceutical as it passes through or settles in parts of the patient's body. After the test has been completed, the technologist views the images on film or on a computer screen to find any additional information to give to the physician, who will interpret the test results.

Although most of their time is spent working directly with patients, nuclear medicine technologists also perform laboratory tests and some administrative work, which involves keeping complete and accurate records.

Places of Employment and Working Conditions   Most nuclear medicine technologists hold jobs in hospitals, but a small number work in medical laboratories, physicians' offices, outpatient clinics, and imaging centers.

Nuclear medicine technologists typically work a 40-hour week. They may be required to work evening or night shifts and may be on call on a rotation basis.

The job can be physically demanding at times. Technologists spend a great deal of time on their feet, and they may have to lift or turn disabled patients.

If workers follow proper safety precautions and wear protective devices, the danger of radiation exposure is minimal. Technologists wear special badges that measure the level of radiation in the area they are working. This measurement very rarely approaches or exceeds established safety levels.

Qualifications, Education, and Training In the past, training was typically given on the job. Now, however, employers prefer to hire technologists who have completed formal training programs. These programs are offered in hospitals, community colleges, universities, and Department of Veterans Affairs medical centers. It is important to realize that there are several different types of programs; they differ in length, prerequisites, class size, cost, and degree awarded upon completion. One-year certificate programs are for health professionals, such as radiologic, ultrasound, or medical technologists, who wish to specialize. Others, who have no previous medical training, may opt for a two-year certificate program, a two-year associate degree program, or a four-year bachelor's degree program. Another important factor to consider in selecting a program is whether it is accredited by the Committee on Allied Health Education and Accreditation (CAHEA). There are 120 CAHEA-accredited programs currently. Many hospitals will hire only those who have completed one of these programs.

Licensure is required in seven states and Puerto Rico. Voluntary certification or registration is available from the American Registry of Radiologic Technologists (ARRT) and the Nuclear Medicine Technology Certification Board (NMTCB). Some employers will give greater consideration to technologists with these credentials.

Potential and Advancement There are currently over 13,000 nuclear medicine technologists. The nuclear medicine technology field is expected to grow faster than the average for all occupations through the year 2005. Excellent employment opportunities exist, and there are reports of a shortage of technologists in this field as enrollment in accredited training programs declines.

Technologists may advance by becoming supervisors or by specializing in an area such as computer analysis or nuclear cardiology. Some technologists become instructors or directors of nuclear medicine technology programs. Others may work in research. Some leave the occupation and become sales representatives with health equipment manufacturing firms or radio-pharmaceutical companies or work as radiation safety officers.

Income   The median annual income of nuclear medicine technologists, based on a 40-hour workweek, was $35,027 in October 1994. Average beginning wages are $28,044 and average maximum is $41,598.

Additional Sources of Information

American Society of Radiologic Technologists
1500 Central Avenue, SE
Albuquerque, NM 87123-3917

Division of Allied Health Education and Accreditation
American Medical Association
535 North Dearborn Street
Chicago, IL 60610

The Society of Nuclear Medicine
136 Madison Avenue
New York, NY 10016

The Society of Nuclear Medicine–Technologist Section
1850 Samuel Morse Dr.
Reston,VA 22090

Occupational Therapist

The Job   This fast-growing field offers personal satisfaction as well as financially rewarding job opportunities. Occupational therapists work with the physically, mentally, and emotionally disabled, helping some to return to normal functions and activities and others to make the fullest use of whatever talents they may have.

Occupational therapists plan and direct educational, vocational, and recreational activities; evaluate capabilities and skills; and plan individual therapy programs, often working as part of a medical team. Their clients are all ages and can range from a stroke patient relearning daily routines such as eating, dressing, and using a telephone to an accident victim learning to use impaired limbs before returning to work.

To restore mobility and dexterity to hands disabled by injury or disease, occupational therapists teach manual and creative skills through the use of crafts such as weaving, knitting, and leather working. They design games and activities especially for children or make special equipment or splints to aid the disabled patient.

Many part-time positions are available for occupational therapists; some occupational therapists work for more than one employer, traveling between job locations and clients.

Most occupational therapists are women, but the number of men entering the field has been increasing. Because there are many opportunities for part-time work, this is a good field for people with family responsibilities.

Related jobs are physical therapist and respiratory therapist.

Places of Employment and Working Conditions   In addition to hospital rehabilitation departments, other types of organizations that employ occupational therapists are rehabilitation centers and nursing homes, schools, mental health centers, schools and camps for handicapped children, state health departments and home care programs, Department of Veterans Affairs hospitals and clinics, psychiatric centers, and schools for children with learning and developmental disabilities. Occupational therapists usually work a 40-hour week, but this may include weekends and evenings. Those who work for schools have regular school hours.

Therapists spend a lot of time on their feet, and they may be subject to back injuries and muscle strains from lifting and moving patients and equipment. Therapists who give home health care may spend several hours a day driving.

Qualifications, Education, and Training   Warmth, patience, and empathy are greatly needed by occupational therapists. Creativity is important in adapting activities to individual needs. Maturity, imagination, manual skills, and the ability to instruct are important as is a sympathetic but objective attitude toward illness and disability.

Anyone considering this career field should have high school science courses, especially biology and chemistry. Courses in health and social studies along with training in crafts are also important. Volunteer work or a summer job in a health care facility can provide valuable exposure to this field.

A bachelor degree or post-bachelor's certificate or degree in occupational therapy is required to practice in this field. Thirty-nine states, Puerto Rico, and the District of Columbia require a license. In 1994, education was offered in 69 bachelor's degree programs; 9 post-bachelor certificate programs; and 19 entry-level master's degree programs.

Graduates of accredited programs take the certification examination of the American Occupational Therapy Association to become a registered occupational therapist (OTR).

Occupational therapy students study physical, biological, and behavioral sciences as well as the application of occupational therapy theory and skills. Students also spend from six to nine months working in hospitals or health agencies to gain clinical experience as an intern.

Potential and Advancement   There are about 54,000 occupational therapists as of 1994, with approximately 40 percent employed in hospitals. Employment in this field is expected to grow substantially because the public is becoming more interested and more knowledgeable about programs for rehabilitating the disabled. Job opportunities will be excellent on the whole through the year 2005; however, as the increasing number of qualified graduates catches up to the number of available jobs, competition for job openings may develop in some geographic areas.

Advancement in this field is usually to supervisory or administrative positions. Advanced education is necessary for those wishing to teach, do research, or advance to top administrative levels.

Income   The median annual salary for occupational therapists, based on a 40-hour week, was $39,634 in 1994. The average minimum was $33,728 and the average maximum was $49,392.

Additional Source of Information

American Occupational Therapy Association
P.O. Box 31220
4720 Montgomery Lane
Bethesda, MD 20824-1220

Pharmacist

The Job   Pharmacists dispense drugs and medicines prescribed by physicians and dentists, advise on the use and proper dosage of prescription and nonprescription medicines, and work in research and marketing positions. Many pharmacists own their own businesses.

The majority of pharmacists work in community pharmacies (drugstores). These range from one-person operations to large retail establishments employing a staff of pharmacists. They answer customers' questions about prescription drugs, such as possible adverse reactions and side effects. They provide information about over-the-counter drugs and make recommendations concerning alternate medications. They also give advice about medical equipment and home health care supplies.

Hospitals and clinics employ pharmacists to dispense drugs and medication to patients, advise the medical staff on the selection and effects of drugs, buy medical supplies, and prepare sterile solutions. In some hospitals, pharmacists also teach nursing classes.

Pharmaceutical manufacturers employ pharmacists in research and development and in sales positions. Drug wholesalers also employ them as sales and technical representatives.

The federal government employs pharmacists in hospitals and clinics of the Department of Veterans Affairs or the U.S. Public Health Service; in the Department of Defense; the Food and Drug Administration; the Department of Health, Education, and Welfare; and in the Drug Enforcement Administration. State and local health agencies also employ pharmacists.

Many community and hospital pharmacists also do consulting work for nursing homes and other health facilities that do not employ a full-time pharmacist.

Places of Employment and Working Conditions   Just about every community has a drugstore employing at least one pharmacist. Most job opportunities, however, are in larger cities and densely populated metropolitan areas.

Pharmacists average about a 44-hour workweek; those who also do consulting work average an additional 15 hours a week. Pharmacists in community pharmacies work longer hours—including evenings and weekends—than those employed by hospitals and other health care institutions, pharmaceutical manufacturers, and drug wholesalers. Some community and hospital pharmacies are open around the clock; pharmacists employed by them may have to work nights, weekends, and holidays.

Pharmacists work in clean, well-lighted and ventilated areas. They use gloves and masks when working with potentially dangerous or sterile pharmaceutical products.

Qualifications, Education, and Training   Prospective pharmacists need an interest in medicine and scientific aptitude and should have orderliness and accuracy, business ability, honesty, and integrity.

Biology and chemistry courses along with some business courses should be taken in high school.

At least five years of study beyond high school are necessary to earn a degree in pharmacy. A few colleges admit pharmacy students immediately following high school, but most require one or two years of prepharmacy college and study in mathematics, basic sciences, humanities, and social sciences. Some programs require the Pharmacy College Admissions Test (PCAT).

Seventy-five colleges of pharmacy are accredited by the American Council on Pharmaceutical Education. Most of these schools award a bachelor of science (B.S.) or a bachelor of pharmacy (B. Pharm.) degree upon completion of the required course of study. About 27 of the schools also offer an advanced degree program leading to a doctor of pharmacy (Pharm.D.) degree. A few schools offer only the Pharm.D. degree. A Pharm.D. normally requires at least six years of study.

A Pharm.D. degree or a master's or Ph.D. degree in pharmacy or a related field is usually required for research, teaching, and administrative positions. In 1994, sixty colleges of pharmacy awarded the Master of Science degree or the Ph.D.

Pharmacists are usually required to serve an internship under the supervision of a registered pharmacist before they can obtain a license to practice. All states, the District of Columbia, and U.S. territories require a license. An applicant usually must have: 1) graduated from an accredited pharmacy college; 2) passed a state board examination; and 3) had a specified amount of practical experience or internship. Many pharmacists are licensed to practice in more than one state, and most states will grant a license without examination to a qualified pharmacist licensed by another state (except California and Florida). Most states require continuing education courses for license renewal.

Post graduate programs are offered in a specific area of pharmacy, such as pediatrics, cardiology, oncology, or hospital pharmacy management.

Potential and Advancement   About 168,000 people work as pharmacists. Job opportunities are expected to be excellent through the year 2005 as the population becomes older and has more pharmaceutical needs. Shortages may even occur in states with high concentrations of the elderly.

Pharmacists employed by chain drugstores may advance to management positions or executive-level jobs within the company. Hospital pharmacists may advance to director of pharmacy service or to other administrative positions.

Pharmacists employed by the pharmaceutical industry have the widest latitude of advancement possibilities because they can advance in management, sales, research, quality control, advertising, production, or packaging. There will be fewer job opportunities, however, with manufacturers than in other areas of pharmacy.

Income   According to a 1994 survey, average base salaries of full-time salaried pharmacists were $53,600 per year. Experienced pharmacists working in chain drugstores earn an average of $54,900 a year; those working in independent drugstores earned an average of $49,000 a year; and hospital pharmacists averaged $54,300 a year.

Additional Sources of Information

American Association of Colleges of Pharmacy
1426 Prince Street
Alexandria, VA 22314

American Society of Hospital Pharmacists
4630 Montgomery Avenue
Bethesda, MD 20814

National Association of Boards of Pharmacy
700 Busse Highway
Park Ridge, IL 60068

Physical Therapist

The Job   At some point in their treatment, accident and stroke victims, handicapped children, and disabled older persons are usually referred by their doctor to a physical therapist. The therapist will design and carry out a program of testing, exercise, massage, or other therapeutic treatment that will increase strength, restore the range of motion, relieve pain, improve the condition of muscles and skin, and prevent or limit permanent physical disability. Physical therapists treat patients with multiple sclerosis, cerebral palsy, nerve injuries, burns, amputations, head injuries, fractures, low back pain, arthritis, and heart disease.

Treatments often include exercise, first by passive exercise and stretching and manipulating stiff joints and unused muscles. Following that treatment, patients are encouraged to use their own muscles, working up to using weights. The goal is to improve strength, balance, coordination, and endurance.

Physical therapists also use electrical stimulation, ultrasound, deep-tissue massage, and hot or cold compresses. They also teach patients how to use crutches, protheses, and wheelchairs.

Physical therapists provide direct patient care and usually do their own evaluation of the patient's needs. The physical therapist works, however, in close cooperation with the physician and any other specialists involved in the care of the patient such as vocational therapists, psychologists, and social workers. In large hospitals and nursing homes, physical therapists may carry out a program designed by the director or assistant director of the physical therapy department rather than develop the program themselves. Some physical therapists specialize in one variety of patient such as children or the elderly or one type of condition such as arthritis, amputations, or paralysis.

Most physical therapists work in hospitals. Nursing homes employ a growing number and also use the services of self-employed therapists. Rehabilitation centers, schools for handicapped children, public health agencies, physicians' offices, and the armed forces all employ physical therapists. Some therapists also work with patients in their own homes or provide instructions to the patient and the patient's family on how to continue therapy at home.

Because this field has so many opportunities for part-time practitioners, it appeals to people with family responsibilities.

Place of Employment and Working Conditions   Physical therapists are employed throughout the country, with the largest number working in cities with large hospitals or medical centers.

Since physical therapy, unlike many other medical procedures, does not have to be provided on a 24-hour basis, most therapists work a 40-hour week. In the case of self-employed and part-time therapists, some evening and weekend work may be required.

Qualifications, Education, and Training   Patience, tact, emotional stability, and the ability to work with people are important for anyone interested in this field. Manual dexterity and physical stamina are also important.

High school students considering this field should take courses in health, biology, social science, mathematics, and physical education. Part-time or volunteer work in the physical therapy department of a hospital can provide a closer look at the work for anyone trying to decide on a career in physical therapy.

There are two types of programs for physical therapy training: a four-year bachelor's degree in physical therapy or an entry-level master's degree program. According to the American Physical Therapy Association (APTA), there were 145 accredited and 39 developing physical therapist programs as of June 1995. Of the accredited programs, 65 offered bachelor's degrees and 80 were master's degree programs. The curriculum starts with courses such as biology, chemistry, and physics, then introduces biomechanics, neuroanatomy, human growth and development, manifestations of disease and trauma, evaluation and assessment techniques, and therapeutic procedures. Students also receive supervised clinical experience in hospitals.

Physical therapists must be licensed. A degree or certificate from an accredited program and a passing grade on a state board examination completes the requirements for obtaining a license. A number of states require continuing education courses to maintain licensure.

Potential and Advancement   There are about 102,000 licensed physical therapists. Employment in the field is expected to expand rapidly as the demand grows for more rehabilitative facilities for accident victims, the elderly, and handicapped children. Opportunities for part-time work will also continue to grow. Growth will also result from advances in medical technology and increased interest in health promotion.

As the number of new graduates in the field catches up with the number of job openings, job competition will probably develop in large population centers. Job opportunities will continue to be good in suburban and rural areas, too.

Advancement in this field depends on experience and advanced education especially for teaching, research, and administrative positions.

Income   According to a survey in October 1994, the median salary of physical therapists based on a 40-hour workweek was $41,288. The average minimum was $35,074 and the average maximum was $51,950.

Additional Source of Information

American Physical Therapy Association
1111 North Fairfax Street
Alexandria, VA 22314-1488

Physical Therapy Assistant

The Job   The purpose of physical therapy is to prevent permanent disability from an injury or illness and to have patients resume their normal activities as soon as possible. Physical therapy assistants work toward these goals by administering to patients therapy plans which are developed by physical therapists.

Physical therapy assistants instruct patients in a wide variety of treatments. They may help them with manual exercise, both weight-bearing and non-weight-bearing, swimming therapy, massage, hot and cold packs, electrical stimulation, paraffin baths, and traction. Assistants carefully monitor the progress of patients during treatment and record this progress, as well as reporting any abnormalities to the physical therapist. They also take measurements of a patient's flexibility and ranges of motion. Some clerical tasks may also be performed by assistants, such as ordering supplies, maintaining patients' records, filling out insurance forms, and answering the phone.

Places of Employment and Working Conditions   The hours
and days that physical therapy assistants work are varied. Some work regular 40-hour work weeks, others work nights and weekends to coincide with patient schedules. Most work in pleasant clinical surroundings.

Physical therapy assistants held over 78,000 jobs in 1994. Over half of them work in hospitals or private physical therapy offices. Some assistants work in sports medicine. The rest work in clinics, schools, nursing homes, and inside patients' homes.

Qualifications, Education, and Training   Physical therapy assistants need patience, empathy, and a willingness to help others. They also need to have a moderate degree of strength due to the physical exertion of lifting patients and standing, stooping, and kneeling for long periods of time.

A physical therapy assistant must earn an associate's degree from an accredited physical therapist program. There are 173 accredited physical therapy assistant programs in the United States, with 54 in developmental progress, according to the American Physical Therapy Association (APTA).

The programs are divided into academic study and course work, and clinical "hands-on" experience. Classes include algebra, anatomy, physiology, biology, and chemistry. Many programs require students to have certification in first aid and CPR before they begin their clinical training. As of 1994, 41 states and Puerto Rico require physical therapy assistants to be licensed or certified.

Potential and Advancement   Physical therapy assistant is expected to be one of the fastest growing careers in health care. Demand will continue to rise as baby boomers age and require more services. The elderly population will also increase. Shortages of physical therapists add to the demand, as physical therapy assistants are an attractive alternative. Many aspects of therapy and treatment can be performed by the licensed assistant.

Income   Starting salaries for physical therapy assistants average approximately $22,500 per year. In private practice, experienced assistants earn upwards of $24,000. Employees of hospitals earn slightly lower salaries, however, as an incentive, some hospitals offer assistants a specified path of advancement and a chance to work with a varied patient population.

Additional Source of Information

American Physical Therapy Association
1111 North Fairfax Street
Alexandria, VA 22314-1488

Radiologic (X-Ray) Technologist

The Job   In the medical field, x-ray pictures (radiographs) are taken by radiologic technologists who operate x-ray equipment. They usually work under the supervision of a radiologist—a physician who specializes in the use and interpretation of x-rays.

There are three specialties within the field of radiologic technology; a radiologic technologist works in all three areas.

The most familiar specialty is the use of x-ray pictures to study and diagnose injury or disease to the human body. In this specialty, the technologist positions the patient and exposes and develops the film. During fluoroscopic examinations (watching the internal movements of the body organs on a screen or monitor), the technologist prepares solutions and assists the physician.

The second specialty area is nuclear medicine technology—the application of radioactive material to aid in the diagnosis and treatment of illness or injury. Working under the direct supervision of a radiologist, the technologist prepares solutions containing radioactive materials that will be absorbed by the patient's internal organs and show up on special cameras or scanners. These materials trace the course of a disease by showing the difference between healthy and diseased tissue.

Radiation therapy—the use of radiation-producing machines to provide therapeutic treatments—is the third specialty. Here, the technologist works under the direct supervision of a radiologist, applying the prescribed amount of radiation for a specified length of time. Most treatments are for cancer patients. They also check patients' reactions for radiation side effects such as nausea, hair loss, and skin irritation. They give instructions and explanations to patients who are likely to be ill.

During all these procedures, the technologist is responsible for the safety and comfort of the patient and must keep accurate and complete records of all treatments. Technologists also schedule appointments and file x-rays and the radiologist's evaluations.

About three-fifths of all radiological technologists work in hospitals. The remainder work in medical laboratories, physicians' and dentists' offices, federal and state health agencies, and public school systems.

Places of Employment and Working Conditions   Radiologic technologists are found in all parts of the country in towns and cities of all sizes. The largest concentrations are in cities with large medical centers and hospitals.

Full-time technologists usually work a 40-hour week. Those employed in hospitals that provide 24-hour emergency coverage have some shift work or may be on call. There are potential radiation hazards in this field, but careful attention to safety procedures and the use of protective clothing and shielding devices provide protection.

Qualifications, Education, and Training   Anyone considering this career should be in good health, emotionally stable, and able to work with people who are injured or ill. The job also requires patience and attention to detail. Formal training is offered in radiography, radiation therapy, and diagnostic medical sonography (ultrasound).

A high school diploma or its equivalent is required for acceptance into an x-ray technology program. Programs approved by the Committee on Allied

Health Education and Accreditation are offered by many hospitals, medical schools affiliated with hospitals, colleges and universities, vocational and technical schools, and the armed forces. The programs vary in length from one to four years; a bachelor's degree in radiologic technology is awarded after completion of the four-year course. Two-year programs are the most prevalent; completion leads to an associate degree.

These training programs include courses in anatomy, physiology, patient care procedures, physics, radiation protection, film processing, medical terminology and ethics, radiographic positioning and exposure, and department administration.

Although registration with the American Registry of Radiologic Technologists is not required for work in this field, it is an asset in obtaining highly skilled and specialized positions. Thirty-one states require radiologic technologists to be licensed. Voluntary registration is offered by the American Registry of Radiologic Technologists (ARRT). To become registered, technologists must be graduates of an accredited program and have passed an examination. With experience and additional training, technologists may become specialists, performing CT scanning, ultrasound, angiography, and magnetic resonance imaging (MRI). Experience can lead to promotion to chief radiologic technologist and department director.

Potential and Advancement   There are about 167,000 radiological technologists at the present time. Employment in this field, as in all medical fields, is expected to expand rapidly because of the importance of this technology to diagnosing and treating disease.

In large x-ray departments, technologists can advance to supervisory positions or quality as instructors in x-ray techniques. There is more opportunity for promotion for those having a bachelor's degree. Most prefer to hire registered technologists.

Income   In 1994, the median earnings for radiologic technologists who worked full time were $29,432. Ten percent earned less than $20,696 and 10 percent earned more than $49,036.

Sick leave, vacation, insurance, and other benefits are usually the same as other employees in the same institution receive.

Additional Sources of Information

American Society of Radiologic Technologists
15000 Central Avenue, SE
Albuquerque, NM 87123-3917

Joint Review Committee on Education in Radiologic Technology
20 N. Wacker Drive
Chicago, IL 60606-2901

Society of Diagnostic Medical Sonographers
12770 Coit Road, Suite 508
Dallas, TX 75251

Recreational Therapist

The Job   Recreational therapy, a fairly new field, uses activities to improve the physical, mental, and emotional health of disabled people. By using activities such as athletic events, dances, arts and crafts, and music, recreational therapists help their patients improve their physical condition, their confidence, their stress management capabilities, and their emotional status. The specific aspects of recreational therapists' jobs, however, depend on their work setting and the type of patients with whom they work.

By talking with patients, their relatives, and other staff members involved in patients' treatment, therapists gather information that will help them determine the best course of treatment for individual patients. Therapists then select a therapeutic activity that complements that patient's interests and enthusiasms.

During the patient's involvement in activities, the therapist closely observes and notes changes and improvements in the patient's condition. The therapist reviews the activity program and determines whether any modifications are necessary as the patient's condition changes or improves. An important part of the therapist's job is recordkeeping—notes on the patient's progress, changes in the treatment plan, staff notes, and discharge notes. These records are used by the medical staff to monitor progress, to make changes, or to end treatment.

Recreational therapists who work in hospitals provide a more active type of treatment. Those working in other settings, such as nursing homes and community centers, tend to emphasize leisure activities more in assisting their patients.

Recreational therapists are also called therapeutic recreation specialists and, in nursing homes, activities directors.

Places of Employment and Working Conditions   Over one-half of all recreational therapists work in hospitals and one-third in nursing homes. Therapists also work in community mental health centers, adult day care programs, correctional facilities, homes for the mentally retarded, community programs, and substance abuse centers. A few therapists are self-employed and oversee programs in nursing homes or community programs on a contract basis.

Working conditions depend on the work setting, facilities, and type of therapy program. Some therapists work in a specially equipped room while others work in a different setting daily or weekly. Therapists usually work a 40-hour week. Working with patients with special needs can be demanding and physically tiring as well if the therapist participates in activities and must lift and carry equipment.

Qualifications, Education, and Training   A desire to help disabled people and patience are important qualities for recreational therapists. Also important are creativity and imagination for determining activities that will meet individual needs.

At this time, hiring requirements vary. For clinical positions, such as those in hospitals, mental health settings, and rehabilitation facilities, a bachelor's degree in therapeutic recreation is usually required. There are over 200 programs in recreational therapy, and around 73 are accredited by the National Council on Accreditation. Most of these are bachelor's degree programs, but some offer associate's or master's degrees. Course work in these programs includes management, professional issues, human anatomy and physiology, abnormal psychology, and characteristics of illnesses and disabilities. In addition, 360 hours of internship under the supervision of a certified therapeutic recreation specialist are required.

In nursing homes, often an associate degree or work experience will qualify an individual for the position of activities director.

A few states monitor this occupation by licensure, certification, or regulation of titles. Typical requirements for licensure include a degree in an accredited therapeutic recreation program, a supervised internship, and passing a state licensing exam. Some employers require individuals to be certified. The National Council for Therapeutic Recreation Certification certifies therapeutic recreation specialists.

Potential and Advancement   There are about 31,000 recreational therapists, and opportunities are expected to grow rapidly through the year 2005 due to increased need for long-term care, physical and psychiatric rehabilitation, and services for the mentally and emotionally disabled.

Job growth will also occur in hospitals. Nursing homes, retirement communities, and adult day care will provide many jobs as the number of people age 75 and older increases. Community programs are expected to grow as well.

To advance, recreational therapists need a master's degree. They may become overseers of programs in larger institutions, teachers, or researchers. Some pursue a doctoral degree.

Income   Several factors affect salaries: employment setting, educational background, experience, and region. The median annual salary for full-time recreational therapists is $31,472. The average annual salary for all recreation therapists in the federal government was about $35,954 in 1995. For recreational therapists with a Ph.D., income could increase to $50,000 to $55,000.

Additional Sources of Information

American Therapeutic Recreation Association
c/o Associated Management Systems
P.O. Box 15215
Hattiesburg, MS 39402-5215

National Council for Therapeutic Recreation Certification
P.O. Box 479
Thiells, NY 10984-0487

National Therapeutic Recreation Society
2775 S. Quincy Street, Suite 300
Arlington, VA 22206-2204

Rehabilitation Counselor

The Job   Rehabilitation counselors work with mentally, physically, and emotionally disabled persons to help them become self-sufficient and productive. Many counselors specialize in one type of disability, such as the mentally retarded, the mentally ill, or the blind. They help people deal with their disabilities. They may counsel people living with birth defects, illness, disease, accidents, or just stress of daily life.

In the course of designing an individual rehabilitation program, the counselor may consult doctors, teachers, and family members to determine the client's abilities and the exact nature of the handicap or disability. He or she will, of course, also work closely with the client. Many counselors discuss training and career options with the client, arrange specialized training and specific job-related training, and provide encouragement and emotional support. They develop and implement a rehabilitation program, which may include training to help the person become more independent and employable. They work toward increasing the client's capacity to adjust and live independently.

An important part of a counselor's work is finding employers who will hire the disabled and the handicapped. Many counselors keep in touch with members of the local business community and try to convince them to provide jobs for the disabled. Once a person is placed in a job, the rehabilitation counselor keeps track of the daily progress of the employee and also confers with the employer about job performance and progress.

The amount of time spent with an individual client depends on the severity of the person's problems and the size of the counselor's case load. Counselors in private organizations can usually spend more time with their clients than those who work for state and local agencies. Less-experienced counselors and counselors who work with the severely disabled usually handle the fewest cases at one time.

Most rehabilitation counselors are employed by state or local rehabilitation agencies. Others work in hospitals or sheltered workshops or are employed by insurance companies and labor unions. The Department of Veterans Affairs employs psychologists who act as rehabilitation counselors.

Related jobs are employment counselor, psychologist, and social worker.

Places of Employment and Working Conditions   Rehabilitation counselors work throughout the country with the largest concentrations in metropolitan areas.

A 40-hour workweek is usual, but attendance at community meetings sometimes requires extra hours. A counselor's working hours are not all spent in the office but include trips to prospective employers, training agencies, and clients' homes.

The work of a counselor can be emotionally exhausting and sometimes discouraging. Counselors must possess a high level of physical and emotional energy to handle the array of problems they encounter.

Most counselors work in pleasant, private offices. Others work in mental health and community agencies.

Qualifications, Education, and Training
Anyone considering this field should have emotional stability, the ability to accept responsibility and work independently, and the ability to motivate and guide other people. Patience is also a necessary characteristic of a rehabilitation counselor because progress often comes slowly over a long period of time.

High school courses in the social sciences should be a part of a college preparatory course.

A bachelor's degree with a major in education, psychology, guidance, or sociology is the minimum requirement. This is sufficient for only a few entry-level jobs. Advanced degrees in psychology, vocational counseling, or rehabilitation counseling are necessary for almost all jobs in this field.

Most rehabilitation counselors work for state and local government agencies and are required to pass the appropriate civil service examinations before appointment to a position. Many private organizations require counselors to be certified; this is achieved by passing the examinations administered by the Commission on Rehabilitation Counselor Certification.

Potential and Advancement
Employment opportunities are expected to be very good, but, since most job openings are in state and local agencies, the employment picture will depend to a great extent on government funding for such services. Under managed care systems, insurance companies will increasingly provide for reimbursement of rehabilitation counselors, which will add to demand. The number of people requiring rehabilitation services will also rise as advances in medical technology continue to save lives. More counseling will also be needed as the elderly population grows.

Experienced rehabilitation counselors can advance to supervisory and administrative jobs.

Income
Median earnings for full-time counselors were about $36,100 in 1994. Self-employed counselors and counselors in group practices generally have the highest earnings.

Additional Sources of Information

American Rehabilitation Counseling Association
5999 Stevenson Avenue
Alexandria, VA 22304

National Rehabilitation Counseling Association
1910 Association Drive
Reston, VA 22091

Council on Rehabilitation Counselor Certification
835 Rohlwing Road, Suite E
Rolling Meadows, IL 60008

Respiratory Therapist

The Job   Respiratory therapists evaluate, treat. and care for patients with breathing disorders. Their role is important and the responsibilities are great.

Respiratory therapists' work includes giving relief to chronic asthma and emphysema sufferers; emergency care in case of heart failure, stroke, drowning, and shock; and treatment of acute respiratory symptoms in cases of head injuries, poisoning, and drug abuse. They must respond swiftly and start treatment quickly because brain damage may occur if a patient stops breathing for three to five minutes, and lack of oxygen for more than nine minutes almost invariably results in death.

In evaluating patients, therapists test the capacity of the lungs and analyze the oxygen and carbon dioxide concentration and pH of the blood. They treat all sorts of patients, including premature babies with underdeveloped lungs to the elderly with diseased lungs. They provide temporary relief to patients with asthma or emphysema, and emergency care for heart failures, strokes, drowning, or shock victims. They also connect patients to respirators, who cannot breath on their own. Respiratory therapists administer aerosol treatments and chest physiotherapy on patients with diseases such as cystic fibrosis.

In addition to respiratory therapists, the field includes *respiratory technicians* and *respiratory assistants*.

Therapists and technicians perform essentially the same duties, with therapists having greater responsibility for supervision and instruction.

Assistants have little contact with the patients; their duties are usually limited to cleaning, sterilizing, and storing the respiratory equipment used by therapists and technicians.

Respiratory therapists and technicians work as part of a health care team following doctors' instructions. They use special equipment and techniques—respirators, positive-pressure breathing machines, and cardiopulmonary resuscitation (CPR)—to treat patients. They are also responsible for keeping records of material costs and charges to patients and maintaining and making minor repairs to equipment. All respiratory therapy workers are trained to observe strict safety precautions in the use and testing of respiratory equipment to minimize the danger of fire.

Most respiratory therapists, technicians, and assistants work in hospitals in respiratory, anesthesiology, or pulmonary medicine departments. Others work for nursing homes, ambulance services, oxygen equipment rental companies, and home health care organizations.

Places of Employment and Working Conditions   Respiratory therapy workers are employed in hospitals throughout the country in communities of all sizes. The largest number of job opportunities exists in large metropolitan areas that support several hospitals or large medical centers. About 90 percent of all respiratory therapists work in hospitals.

Respiratory therapy workers usually work a 40-hour week and may be required to work evenings, nights, or weekends. Respiratory therapists spend much of their working time on their feet and experience a great deal of stress. They must be careful when working with gases, and they run the risk of catching an infectious disease.

Qualifications, Education, and Training   Anyone interested in entering this field should enjoy working with people and have a patient, sensitive, and understanding manner. The ability to follow instructions and work as a member of a team is important. Manual dexterity and some mechanical ability are necessary in the operation and maintenance of the sometimes complicated respiratory therapy equipment.

High school students interested in this field should take courses in health, biology, mathematics, physics, and bookkeeping.

Formal training in respiratory therapy is necessary for entering the field. There are about 275 institutions that offer programs approved by the Committee on Allied Health Education and Accreditation (CAHEA). All these programs require a high school diploma. Courses may vary from two to four years and include both classroom and clinical work. Students study anatomy and physiology, chemistry, physics, microbiology, and mathematics. A bachelor's degree is awarded to those completing a four-year program, with an associate degree awarded for some of the two-year programs.

Thirty-eight states license respiratory therapists. The National Board for Respiratory Care offers voluntary certification and registration to graduates of schools accredited by the CAAEP. Respiratory technicians can receive certification as a *certified respiratory technician* (CRTT) if they have completed a CAHEA-approved technical training program and have one year of experience. They must pass a single written examination. All respiratory technicians are certified as CRTTs. After two years of clinical experience, respiratory therapists are eligible to take the registry exam to become a *registered respiratory therapist* (RRT).

Potential and Advancement
There are currently about 73,000 respiratory therapists. The field is growing rapidly. Growth of health care services in general and the expanding use of respiratory therapy and equipment by hospitals, ambulance services, and nursing homes make this a good job opportunity area, as more and more respiratory specialists are hired to release nurses and other personnel from respiratory therapy duties.

Advancement in this field depends on experience and additional education. Respiratory assistants can advance to the technician or therapist level by completing the required courses; technicians can advance by achieving certification or completing education and testing requirements for the therapist level.

Respiratory therapists can be promoted to assistant chief or chief therapist. With graduate study they can qualify for teaching positions. Supervisory positions and those in intensive care require the RRT.

Income
Median annual earnings for respiratory therapists working full time in 1994 were $30,212. The average minimum salary was $25,978 and the average maximum was $38,233.

Additional Sources of Information

American Association for Respiratory Care
11030 Ables Lane
Dallas, TX 75229

The National Board for Respiratory Care, Inc.
8310 Nieman Road
Lenexa, KS 66214

Joint Review Committee for Respiratory Therapy Education
1701 W. Euless Boulevard, Suite 300
Euless, TX 76040

Social Worker

The Job   Social work is a vast field, and social workers have tremendously varied responsibilities. They help people deal with a large range of problems. They help individuals and families cope with inadequate housing, unemployment, mental illness, disability, debilitating illness, substance abuse, and unwanted pregnancy. They also help people deal with financial mismanagement, lack of job skills, antisocial behavior, and family problems such as child, spousal, or elderly abuse.

Most social workers specialize in a specific clinical field such as child welfare and family services, mental health, schools, or counseling. Others are employed in community organizations, research, or administration. Health care social workers help patients and their families cope with chronic, acute, or terminal illnesses. They may organize support groups for families of patients suffering from cancer, AIDS, Alzheimer's disease, or other illnesses.

Those social workers who work in schools diagnose students' problems, arrange needed services, counsel children, and help plan for their needs. Occupational social workers work with personnel departments and help employees battle stress, job-related pressures, and personal problems that are affecting the quality of their work.

Some social workers specialize in gerontology and run support groups for the adult children of sick parents; advise the elderly about choices in housing, health care, and transportation; and coordinate these services. Social workers in child welfare or family services may counsel children who have difficulties, arrange for adoptions, find foster homes, and develop plans for treatments.

Places of Employment and Working Conditions   Most social workers work in voluntary social service agencies, community and religious organizations, hospitals, nursing homes, and home health agencies. Nearly 40 percent of the jobs are in state, county, or municipal government agencies.

Social workers spend most of their time in an office or residential facility. Although most work a 40-hour week, some evening and weekend hours are necessary to meet with clients, attend meetings, and handle emergencies. Although satisfying, social work can be emotionally draining and stressful due to understaffing and large caseloads.

Qualifications, Education, and Training   Social workers need to be sensitive and compassionate to people and their problems. Maturity and

objectivity are also extremely important. They must be able to handle responsibility, work independently, and maintain good relations with their clients, families, and colleagues.

A bachelor's degree is the minimum requirement for most positions. A bachelor's degree in psychology, sociology, or another related field may satisfy some job requirements that ask for a BSW. A master's degree is generally necessary for positions in health and mental health settings. Public agencies may require a MSW as well. Supervisory, administrative, and staff training positions require a master's degree. A doctorate is required in college and university teaching positions and research appointments.

The Council on Social Work Education accredited 383 BSW programs and 117 MSW programs in 1994. There are also fifty-six doctoral programs for the Ph.D. in social work and DSW (Doctor of Social Work). BSW programs prepare graduates for direct service positions, such as case worker. An MSW prepares the graduate to perform assessments, manage cases, and supervise other workers. Master's programs usually take two years and include nine hundred hours of supervised field experience, or internship.

Since 1993, all states and the District of Columbia have had licensing, certification, or registration laws regarding social work practice and the use of titles. Voluntary certification is offered by the National Association of Social Workers and grants the title ACSW (Academy of Certified Social Workers) or ACBSW (Academy of Certified Baccalaureate Social Workers). For clinical social workers, who are granted the title QCSW (Qualified Clinical Social Worker), professional credentials include listing in the *NASW Register of Clinical Social Workers*.

Advanced credentials include the NASW Diplomate in Clinical Social Work, and School Social Work Specialist. An advanced credential is also offered by the *Directory of Clinical Social Workers*.

Potential and Advancement   Social workers may advance to supervisor, program manager, assistant director, or executive director of an agency or department. Both experience and a MSW are necessary for advancement. Other career options for social workers include teaching, research, and consulting.

Income   Social workers with MSW degrees had a median earnings of $30,000 in 1993. In hospitals, social workers who worked full time averaged $33,000 in 1994, with a maximum salary of $40,100. The average annual salary for all social workers in the federal government in nonsupervisory, supervisory, and managerial positions was about $44,000 in 1995.

Additional Sources of Information

National Association of Social Workers
IC-Career Information
750 First Street, NE, Suite 700
Washington, DC 20002-4241

National Network for Social Work Managers, Inc.
1316 New Hampshire Avenue, NW, Suite 602
Washington, DC 20036

Council on Social Work Education
1600 Duke Street
Alexandria, VA 22314-3421

Speech Pathologist and Audiologist

The Job   Speech pathologists and audiologists evaluate speech, language, voice, fluency, and hearing disorders and provide treatment. Speech pathologists work with children and adults who cannot make speech sounds and have voice disorders because of hearing loss, brain injury, cleft palate, mental retardation, emotional problems, or foreign dialect. They also treat people with speech rhythm and fluency problems, such as stuttering, and people with speech quality problems, such as inappropriate pitch or harsh voice. They also may work with people with oral motor problems that cause eating and swallowing difficulties.

Speech pathologists use special instruments and oral and written tests to determine the extent of impairment. They record and analyze speech irregularities. For individuals with no or little speech, they select alternative communication systems including sign language and automated devices and teach their clients how to use them. Audiologists assess and treat hearing problems. They use audiometers and other testing devices to measure hearing loss, the ability to distinguish between sounds, and the loudness at which a person begins to hear. Speech and audiology are so interrelated that expertise in one field requires thorough knowledge of both.

Almost half of all speech pathologists and audiologists work in public schools; colleges and universities employ large numbers in teaching and research. The remainder work in hospitals, clinics, government agencies, industry, and private practice.

Places of Employment and Working Conditions   Speech pathologists and audiologists are employed throughout the country with most of them located in urban areas.

Speech pathologists and audiologists usually work at a desk or table in an office setting. While the job is not physically strenuous, it does require concentration and attention to detail and can be mentally exhausting. Some speech pathologists and audiologists work at several different facilities and spend a lot of time traveling. The work can be demanding. Most work 40 hours per week

Qualifications, Education, and Training   Patience is an extremely important characteristic for anyone who wants to work in this field since progress is usually very slow. The therapist must also be able to encourage and motivate the clients, who are often frustrated by the inability to speak properly. Objectivity and the ability to take responsibility and work with detail are also necessary.

High school should include a strong science background.

A bachelor's degree with a major in speech and hearing or in a related field such as education or psychology is the usual preparation for graduate work.

Most jobs in this field require a master's degree. Graduate study includes supervised clinical training as well as advanced study. By the year 2000, a doctoral degree may be required for most jobs.

About 230 colleges and universities offered master's degree program in 1995. Those with a master's degree can acquire the Certificate of Clinical Competence (CCC) offered by the American Speech-Language-Hearing Association. To earn the CCC, a person must have a master's degree, 300 to 375 hours of supervised clinical experience, complete a nine-month postgraduate internship, and pass a written examination. Certification is usually necessary to advance professionally.

In 45 states, speech pathologists and audiologists must be licensed.

Potential and Advancement   There are about 85,000 speech pathologists and audiologists. The field is expected to grow as a result of population growth among those age 75 and older, the trend toward earlier recognition and treatment of hearing and language problems in children, recent laws requiring services for the handicapped, and the expanded coverage of Medicare and Medicaid programs. Any decreases in government-funded programs could change this employment picture. Increases in school enrollments will add to growth.

If present trends continue, the increasing number of degrees being awarded in this field may cause some job competition in large metropolitan areas. Job opportunities will continue to be good in smaller cities and towns.

Those with only a bachelor degree will find very limited job opportunities; advancement will be possible only for those with graduate degrees.

Income   According to a 1994 survey, the median annual salary for full-time certified speech pathologists with one to three years experience was about $31,000. Those with 16 years or more earned a salary of $42,430. Those employed by hospitals earned a median salary of $35,372.

Additional Sources of Information

American Speech-Language-Hearing Association
10801 Rockville Pike
Rockville, MD 20852

American Academy of Audiology
1735 N. Lynn Street, #900
Arlington, VA 22209

Surgical Technologist

The Job   Surgical technologists, also called surgical technicians or operating room technicians, provide general assistance to doctors and nurses before, during, and after a surgical procedure. Before an operation, surgical technologists prepare the operating room by making sure that surgical instruments, equipment, sterile linens, and fluids are in place. They also may get patients ready for surgery by washing, shaving, and disinfecting areas on which the surgeon will operate. They then transport patients to the operating room, position them on the operating table, and help drape them. They also observe patients' vital signs, check charts, and help the surgical team scrub and put on gowns, masks, and gloves.

During surgery, they assist surgeons by passing them sterile instruments and other supplies. They may be required to hold retractors, cut sutures, and help count equipment used during the surgery such as sponges and needles. Specimens taken for laboratory analysis must be prepared, cared for, and disposed of—often the surgical technologists may have to operate some of the equipment used during the surgery, such as sterilizers, lights, or suction machines.

After a surgery, technologists take patients to the recovery room and assist nurses in seeing that the operating room is restocked with the necessary supplies.

Places of Employment and Working Conditions   Most surgical technologists work in hospitals or facilities where there are operating rooms, delivery rooms, or emergency rooms. The shift to outpatient and ambulatory surgery provides jobs in clinics and offices of physicians.

Technologists work in a clean, well-lighted, cool environment. The job may be physically and mentally demanding—technologists sometimes must stay on their feet and remain alert and able to concentrate for surgeries that sometimes last long hours. At times they may be exposed to communicable diseases and unpleasant sights, odors, and materials.

Technologists usually work 40-hour, five-day weeks. Since emergency surgery is performed around the clock, technologists may have to be on call during weekends and evenings.

Qualifications, Education, and Training   Those interested in being surgical technologists must have good manual dexterity for handling instruments. Technologists must be conscientious, able to concentrate, and able to work well under pressure.

Almost all technologists are trained in formal education programs offered by community and junior colleges, vocational and technical institutes, or hospitals. There are currently around 200 programs, and 147 are accredited by the Committee on Allied Health Education and Accreditation of the American Medical Association. Most programs last from 9 to 24 months. Community college programs last two years; those who complete a two-year program are granted associate's degrees.

Students in these programs receive instruction in anatomy and physiology, microbiology, pharmacology, and medical terminology. Students also learn how to care for patients during surgery; sterilization techniques; and how to handle certain drugs, equipment, solutions, and supplies.

Technologists may obtain voluntary professional certification from the Liason Council on Certification for the Surgical Technologist by graduating from a formal program and passing a national certification exam. They may then use the designation *certified surgical technologist* (CST). Continuing education or reexamination is required every six years.

Potential and Advancement   There are about 46,000 technologists currently, and this field is expected to grow rapidly through the year 2005. The rate of surgery is expected to climb as a large percentage of the population grows older, technological advances allow for more surgical intervention for numerous conditions, and insurance companies offer more widespread coverage for surgical care.

Many technologists advance by leaving the field altogether and becoming salespeople; consumer relations specialists; or managers for insurance companies, sterile supply services, or operating equipment firms. They may become instructors in surgical technology programs or, with more education, become registered nurses. Technologists may also advance by specializing in a particular area of surgery, such as neurosurgery or open heart surgery.

Income   The average annual salary for surgical technologists was about $22,285 in 1994, with more experienced workers earning about $27,690. Salaries vary according to geographical location, with workers on the East and West coasts earning more. Technologists employed by surgeons rather than hospitals tend to earn more.

Additional Sources of Information

Association of Surgical Technologists
7108-C S. Alton Way
Englewood, CO 80112

Liaison Council on Certification for the Surgical Technologist
7108-C S. Alton Way
Englewood, CO 80112

Eye Care

Ophthalmic Laboratory Technician
Ophthalmologist
Optician (Dispensing)
Optometrist

Eye Care   Eyes and vision are an extremely important aspect of each individual's general health and quality of life. Careers in eye care encompass the treatment of eye problems and the prevention of diseases of the eyes and surrounding structures. General eye care also entails education of the population to new treatments of vision problems and the prevention of diseases of the eye. Careers in eye care can be very satisfying, as vision is such an important part of each patient's life.

Careers described in this section include ophthalmologist, optometrist, ophthalmic laboratory technician, and optician.

Ophthalmic Laboratory Technician

The Job   After an optometrist or ophthalmologist has examined a patient's eyes and prescribed corrective lenses, the prescription is sent to a laboratory where an ophthalmic laboratory technician, also called a manufacturing optician, optical mechanic, or optical goods worker, makes the lenses according to specifications and fits them into frames to produce finished glasses.

The order sent by the optometrist or ophthalmologist specifies the degree of curvature of the lens that will improve the patient's vision. The technician marks on a blank lens where the curves should be ground, sets the dials on a lens grinder for the correct degree of curvature, and starts and monitors the machine. After the lens has been ground, the technician finishes it by smoothing out the rough edges and polishing it.

The technician then uses special equipment to make sure the lenses meet the specifications on the prescription. The lenses are then cut and beveled to fit the frame, and the technician assembles lenses and frame into a finished pair of glasses.

In small laboratories, a technician will handle each step in this process; in larger laboratories, technicians may specialize in one particular step.

Places of Employment and Working Conditions   About half of all ophthalmic laboratory technicians work in retail stores that manufacture prescription glasses and sell them directly to the public. Most of the rest work in optical laboratories, and a few work for optometrists and ophthal-mologists.

Most technicians work a 40-hour, five-day week, with some weekend and evening hours. Their working environment is usually clean, well lighted, and quiet. They may be required to stand most of the time.

Qualifications, Education, and Training   Ophthalmic laborato-ry technicians must be detail oriented, able to follow instructions, and have good manual dexterity. Employers usually prefer to hire workers with a high school diploma.

Almost all technicians receive their training on the job, but there are a few formal programs in vocational-technical institutes and trade schools. Those trained on the job go through a 6- to 18-month training program, first learn-ing the most basic tasks and gradually learning more difficult tasks.

Potential and Advancement   There are currently about 26,000 oph-thalmic laboratory technicians, and the field is expected to grow rapidly through the year 2000. Retail optical chains will offer the most new jobs.

Technicians usually advance by becoming supervisors or managers. Some receive further education and become dispensing opticians.

Income   Most beginning technicians earn between $10,000 and $15,000 a year. Trainees usually are paid minimum wage and are given increases as they gain skills. Those with three to five years of experience averaged $17,913; six to ten years, $22,873; and over eleven years $23,980.

Additional Source of Information

Commission on Opticianry Accreditation
10111 Martin Luther KIng, Jr., Highway, Suite 110
Bowie, MD 20715

Ophthalmologist

The Job   Ophthalmologists are also called eye physician-surgeons. They are qualified allopathic and osteopathic physicians who have completed additional specialized training in the treatment of eye disease and disorders. They treat a full range of eye problems including vision deficiencies, injuries, infections, and other disorders with medicines, therapy, corrective lenses, or surgery. Their job is distinct from that of optometrists and opticians, who are not physicians and treat only vision problems.

Most ophthalmologists are in private practice. Others are employed by hospitals and clinics, medical schools and research foundations, federal and state agencies, and the armed forces.

Related jobs are optometrist, dispensing optician, allopathic physician, and osteopathic physician.

Places of Employment and Working Conditions   Ophthalmologists work in all areas of the country. Those who are osteopathic physicians are concentrated in the areas that have osteopathic facilities—mainly in Florida, Michigan, Pennsylvania, New Jersey, Ohio, Texas, and Missouri. The workweek for ophthalmologists is from 35 to 50 hours. Those involved in general patient care are always on call for emergencies.

Qualifications, Education, and Training   Information on the training and licensing requirements for allopathic and osteopathic physicians is contained in the sections on allopathic and osteopathic physicians.

An additional three to five years of residency in an accredited ophthalmology program must be completed by doctors who wish to specialize in this field. Candidates for the specialty must then pass the certification examination of the American Board of Ophthalmology or the American Osteopathic Board of Ophthalmology.

Potential and Advancement   The demand for ophthalmologists will continue to grow as the population grows. Greater interest in eye care, the growing number of senior citizens, and the increase in health insurance plans will all add to the need for qualified practitioners of this medical specialty. New technologies, such as laser surgery, will provide great advances in eye care and vision.

Income   Ophthalmologists who start a private practice face a few lean years until the practice is established. In addition, a sizable investment in specialized equipment is necessary. Earnings during this early period may barely meet expenses.

As a practice grows, earnings usually increase substantially. Average annual earnings for all ophthalmologists are in the $150,000 range with some earning even more. In general, ophthalmologists in private practice earn more than those in salaried positions. Ophthalmology is considered to be a surgical subspecialty, and those performing many surgeries can earn upward of $200,000 per year.

Additional Sources of Information

American Academy of Ophthalmology
655 Beach Street
P.O. Box 7424
San Francisco, CA 94120

American Medical Association
535 North Dearborn Street
Chicago, IL 60610

Optician, Dispensing

The Job   Over half the people in the United States use some form of corrective lenses (eyeglasses or contact lenses). These corrective lenses are prepared and fitted by dispensing opticians, who are also called ophthalmic dispensers. Working with the prescription received from an ophthalmologist (eye physician) or optometrist, the dispensing optician provides the customer with the appropriate eyeglasses. He or she measures the customer's face, aids in the selection of the appropriate lens size and material and frame color and style, prepares a work order that gives ophthalmic laboratory technicians the information needed to grind and insert lenses into a frame, and fits the completed eyeglasses.

In many states, dispensing opticians also fit contact lenses, which requires even more skill, care, and patience than the preparation and fitting of eyeglasses. Opticians measure the corneas of the customer's eyes and, following the ophthalmologist's or optometrist's prescription, prepare specifications for the contact lens manufacturer. The optician will instruct the customer on how to insert, remove, and care for the contact lenses and will provide follow-up attention during the first few weeks.

Some dispensing opticians specialize in the fitting of artificial eyes and cosmetic shells to cover blemished eyes. Some also do their own lens grinding.

Most dispensing opticians work for retail optical shops or other retail stores with optical departments. Ophthalmologists and optometrists who sell glasses directly to patients also employ dispensing opticians, as do hospitals and eye clinics. A number of dispensing opticians operate their own retail shops and sell other optical goods such as binoculars, magnifying glasses, and sunglasses.

Places of Employment and Working Conditions   Dispensing opticians are located throughout the United States with most employed in large cities and in the more populous states. Working conditions are usually quiet and clean with a workweek of five or six days. Dispensing opticians who own their own businesses usually work longer hours than those employed by retail shops or by ophthalmologists and optometrists. They work indoors in attractive, well-lighted, and well-ventilated offices. They may work in medical offices or stores. Opticians spend a lot of time with their clients and much time is spent on their feet.

Qualifications, Education, and Training   The ability to do precision work is essential for anyone planning a career as a dispensing optician. Patience, tact, and the ability to deal with people are other valuable assets.

Applicants for entry-level jobs in this field need a high school diploma with courses in the basic sciences. High school courses in physics, algebra, geometry , and mechanical drawing are especially valuable.

Most opticians acquire their skills through on-the-job training. A small number of dispensing opticians learn their trade in the armed forces. In addition, large manufacturers of contact lenses offer nondegree courses in lens-fitting.

In 1995, forty programs offered a two-year full-time course in optical fabricating and dispensing which led to an associate degree; 24 were accredited by the Commission on Opticianry Accreditation. Students learn optical mathematics, optical physics, and the use of precision measuring instruments.

Apprenticeship programs lasting from two to five years are also available. In these programs, the students study optometric technical subjects and basic office management and sales and work directly with patients in the fitting of eyeglasses and contact lenses.

Dispensing opticians must be licensed in at least 22 states. Specific requirements vary from state to state but generally include minimum standards of education and training along with a written or practical examination.

Potential and Advancement
About 49,000 persons work as dispensing opticians. Employment opportunities in this field are expected to grow steadily along with the population. Increased health insurance coverage, Medicare services, and state programs to provide eye care to low-income families—along with current fashion trends, which encourage sales of more than one pair of glasses to individual buyers—will add to the demand for dispensing opticians. The number of middle-aged and elderly persons is increasing. This group increasingly needs corrective lenses. New lens treatments such as photochromatic lenses, new bifocal toric lenses, extended wear and disposable contact lenses will add to the growing response of the population to corrected vision wear.

Many dispensing opticians go into the business for themselves. Others advance to positions in the management of retail optical stores or become sales representatives for wholesalers or manufacturers of eyeglasses or contact lenses.

Income
Earnings for dispensing opticians vary a great deal. Highest earnings are in those states that require licensure. The average annual earnings for dispensing opticians were $26,500 a year in 1994. Managers averaged about $30,400.

Additional Sources of Information

National Academy of Opticianry
10111 Martin Luther King, Jr., Highway, Suite 112
Bowie, MD 20720-4299

Opticians Association of America
10341 Democracy Lane
P.O. Box 10110
Fairfax, VA 22030

Optometrist

The Job Over half of the U.S. population wear corrective lenses (eyeglasses or contact lenses). Before obtaining lenses, people need an eye examination and a prescription to obtain the correct lenses for their particular eye problem. Optometrists (doctors of optometry) provide the bulk of this care, and examine eyes to diagnose vision problems and eye diseases.

In addition to handling vision problems, optometrists also check for disease. When evidence of disease is found, an optometrist refers the patient to the appropriate medical practitioner. Optometrists also check depth and color perception and the ability to focus and coordinate the eyes. They may prescribe corrective eye exercises or other treatments that do not require surgery. Optometrists can utilize medications for diagnosis, while in 46 states they can also treat eye diseases and use topical and oral drugs.

Some optometrists specialize in work with children or the aged or work only with the partially sighted who must wear microscopic or telescopic lenses. Industrial eye-safety programs also are an optometric specialty. A few optometrists are engaged in teaching and research. Some provide postoperative care to cataract and other eye surgery patients.

Although most optometrists are in private practice, many others are in partnerships or in group practice with other optometrists or with other physicians as part of a health care team. Some work in retail vision chain stores. Many combine private, group, or partnership practice with work in specialized hospitals and eye clinics.

Some optometrists serve as commissioned officers in the armed forces. Others are consultants to engineers specializing in safety or lighting; to educators in remedial reading; and to health advisory committees of federal, state, and local governments.

Places of Employment and Working Conditions Most optometrists are in general practice. Some teach, do research, or consult. Their private offices are clean, well-lighted, and well-ventilated, comfortable and attractive. Although most optometrists work in California, Illinois, New York, Pennsylvania, and Ohio, opportunities exist in towns and cities of all sizes.

Most self-employed optometrists can set their own work schedule but often work longer than 40 hours a week. Because the work is not physically strenuous, optometrists can practice past the normal retirement age. Many work evenings and weekends to suit the needs of patients.

Qualifications, Education, and Training Because most optometrists are self-employed, anyone planning on a career in this field needs business ability and self-discipline in addition to the ability to deal effectively with people.

High school preparation should emphasize science, and business courses are also helpful.

Six to eight years of college are required to become an optometrist. Two to four years of college or university study are required for admission to an accredited optometry school, where the doctor of optometry degree is awarded after successful completion of a four-year program. The two to four years of preoptometrical study should include English, mathematics, physics, chemistry, and biology or zoology. Some schools also require psychology, social studies, literature, philosophy, and foreign languages. Most optometry students, however, have a bachelor's degree.

Admission to optometry schools is highly competitive. Because the number of qualified applicants exceeds the available places, applicants need superior grades in preoptometric courses to increase their chances of acceptance by one of the 17 schools of optometry approved by the Council on Optometric Education of the American Optometric Association. Applicants must also take the Optometry Admissions Test (OAT).

Optometrists who wish to advance in a specialized field of optometry may study for a master's or Ph.D. degree in visual science, physiological optics, neurophysiology, public health, health administration, health information and communication, or health education. Career officers in the armed forces also have an opportunity to work toward advanced degrees and to do research.

One-year postgraduate clinical residency programs are available for optometrists who wish to specialize in family practice, pediatric or geriatric optometry, vision therapy, contact lenses, hospital-based optometry, or ocular disease.

Potential and Advancement In 1994, there were about 37,000 practicing optometrists, many of them in private practice. Employment opportunities are expected to grow steadily through the year 2005. Increasing coverage of optometric services by health insurance, greater recognition of the importance of good vision, and the growing population—especially older people who are most likely to need eyeglasses—should contribute to an increase in the demand for optometrists. The oldest age group will need more care due to increased likelihood of cataracts, glaucoma, diabetes, and hypertension.

Income   Incomes for optometrists vary greatly depending on location, specialization, and factors such as private or group practice. New optometry graduates average $55,500 in their first year.

Experienced optometrists average about $80,000 a year with those associate or partnership practices earning substantially more than those in private practice.

Additional Sources of Information

American Optometric Association, Educational Services
243 North Lindbergh Boulevard
St. Louis, MO 63141

Association of Schools and Colleges of Optometry
6110 Executive Boulevard, Suite 690
Rockville, MD 20852

Animal Care

Veterinarian
Veterinary Assistant

Animal Care   Careers in animal care offer a very different opportunity in the health care field, and that is to work with all kinds of animals on their health needs. Dealing with animals also involves people skills, as each pet has an owner who cares for his or her animal or pet. Treating animals entails many different skills and abilities from that of human health care. Veterinarians and their assistants must be good diagnosticians and have compassion for their fellow creatures. Careers in animal care can be very rewarding and satisfying.

The careers of the veterinarian and veterinary assistant are explored in this section.

Veterinarian

The Job   Doctors of veterinary medicine diagnose, treat, and control diseases and injuries of animals. They treat animals in hospitals and clinics and on farms and ranches. They diagnose medical problems, dress wounds, set broken bones, perform surgery, prescribe and administer medicines, and vaccinate animals against diseases.

Veterinarians also contribute to human health. They are engaged in research, food safety inspection, and education. Some work with physicians and medical scientists on research to prevent and treat diseases in humans.

Veterinarians help prevent the outbreak and spread of animal diseases, some of which, like rabies, can be transmitted to humans. Others specialize in epidemiology or animal pathology.

In the army, the air force, and the U.S. Public Health Service, veterinarians are commissioned officers. Other federally employed veterinarians work for the Department of Agriculture.

Places of Employment and Working Conditions   Veterinarians are located throughout the country—in rural areas, small towns, cities, and suburban areas.

While most familiar to the general public are those veterinarians who treat small animals and pets exclusively, others specialize in the health and breeding of cattle, horses, and other farm animals. Veterinarians are also employed by federal and state public health programs where they function as meat and poultry inspectors. Others teach at veterinary colleges; do research on animal foods, diseases, and drugs; or take part in medical research for the treatment of human diseases. Veterinarians are also employed by zoos, large animal farms, horse racing stables, and drug manufacturers.

Working hours are often long and irregular, and those who work primarily with farm animals must work outdoors in all kinds of weather. In the course of their work, all veterinarians are exposed to animal bites, kicks, and scratches, disease, and infection.

Veterinarians usually treat pets in hospitals and clinics. Most work at least 40 hours per week, often 50 or more, and may work nights and weekends.

Qualifications, Education, and Training   A veterinarian needs the ability to get along with animals and should have an interest in science. Physical stamina and a certain amount of strength are also necessary. A veterinarian also needs manual dexterity, ability to make quick decisions, and patience.

High school students interested in this field should emphasize science courses, especially biology. Summer jobs that involve the care of animals can provide valuable experience.

The veterinary degree program (D.V.M or V.M.D.) requires a minimum of six years of college—at least two years of preveterinary study with emphasis on physical and biological sciences followed by a four-year professional degree program. Most successful applicants complete four years of college before entering the professional program.

There are only 27 accredited colleges of veterinary medicine, many of them state supported. Admission to all of these schools is highly competitive with many more qualified applicants than the schools can accept. Successful applicants need preveterinary college grades of B or better, especially in science courses; part-time work or summer job experience working with animals is a plus. State-supported colleges usually give preference to residents of the state and to applicants from nearby states or regional areas.

The course of study in veterinary colleges is rigorous. It consists of classroom work and practical experience in diagnosing and treating animal diseases, surgery, laboratory work in anatomy and biochemistry, and other scientific and medical studies. Veterinarians who intend to teach or do research usually go on to earn a master's degree in pathology, physiology, or bacteriology or a Ph.D.

All states and the District of Columbia require veterinarians to be licensed. Licensing requires a doctor of veterinary medicine degree from an accredited college and passing a written state board of proficiency examination. Some states will issue licenses without examination to veterinarians licensed by another state.

Potential and Advancement   There are about 56,000 active veterinarians, most of them in private practice. Employment opportunities for veterinarians are excellent primarily because of growth in the population of companion animals—horses, dogs, and other pets—and an increase in veterinary research. The growing emphasis on scientific methods of breeding and raising livestock and poultry as well as an increase in public health and disease control programs will also contribute to the demand for veterinarians.

Income   The income of veterinarians in private practice varies greatly depending on type of practice, years of experience, and size and location of community. They usually have higher incomes, however, than veterinarians in salaried positions. The average starting salary for veterinarians is $30,694 a year. More experienced veterinarians' salaries range from $40,000 to $60,000 a year. The average income of veterinarians in private practice was $59,188 in 1994.

Additional Sources of Information

American Veterinary Medical Association
1931 North Meacham Road, Suite 100
Schaumburg, IL 60173-4360

Association of American Veterinary Medical Colleges
1101 Vermont Avenue, NW, Suite 710
Washington, DC 20005

Veterinary Assistant

The Job   The veterinary assistant is like a primary care nurse in human hospitals. Busy veterinarians rely on their assistants to keep a constant watch over the animals in their care. Veterinary assistants prepare animals for surgery, watch as animals recover from surgery, check dressings and perform other postoperative procedures, give animals medication, and observe the animals' attitude and notify a doctor if anything is out of the ordinary. They also clean constantly to maintain a sanitary environment.

Veterinary assistants with formal training may perform medical tests for use in the animals' treatment and diagnosis of disease. They will clean and sterilize instruments and take blood and tissue samples for laboratory testing. Executing laboratory tests such as urinalyses and blood counts may also be part of the job description. They will initially weigh the animals, examine animals for the veterinarians, and record on charts.

Places of Employment and Working Conditions

Most veterinary assistants work directly under a veterinarian in his or her private office. Others work in boarding kennels, animal shelters, grooming shops, zoological parks, stables, parks, and local, state, and federal agencies.

Working conditions can vary according to the place of employment. Many veterinary assistants work in pleasant, well-lighted and ventilated, sanitary offices for a 40-hour work week. Others work outdoors in all kinds of weather. Some work night shifts and weekends.

Qualifications, Education, and Training

Veterinary assistants must love animals and get satisfaction from working with and helping animals. They need to be in good health and physical condition. They must be emotionally stable, responsible, and caring.

People who work with animals can be exposed to bites, scratches, kicks, and diseases from the animals they attend. Hours can sometimes be irregular, as animals need to be fed and cared for 24 hours a day. Some weekends and evening hours may be necessary.

Most animal caretakers are extensively trained on the job. Training may be through a veterinarian or a state humane society. Some veterinary assistants have postsecondary education, such as trade school or junior college. Some community or technical colleges offer an associate degree, which involves one to two years of course work and hands-on experience.

Potential and Advancement

Job opportunities will be good in the next decade. As the economy and population expands, pet ownership grows. The number of dogs and cats has increased significantly over the last ten years, and is expected to increase. More animals mean more caretakers to provide services for the animals.

Advancement varies with the employment setting. Experience and further training usually mean higher wages and more extensive duties.

Income   The average animal caretaker earns between $211 and $368 weekly. The top 10 percent earned a weekly salary of $536.

Additional Sources of Information

American Veterinary Association
1931 N. Meacham Road, Suite 100
Schaumburg, IL 60173-4360

Animal Caretakers Information
The Human Society of the United States
2100 L Street, NW
Washington, DC 20037

Science, Education, and Research

Biomedical Engineer
Medical Scientist
Research Laboratory Technician

Science, Education, and Research Careers in science, education, and research differ somewhat from many of the other health careers in this book. There is little or no patient contact. Very few people in these careers work in a hospital or primary care center. The requirements for these careers include computer knowledge, engineering skills, proficiency in laboratory machinery and equipment, research techniques, and creative and writing abilities. People involved in this area of health care are searching for new methods, new facts, new preventive measures, and new treatments for health problems. Teaching, another important part of the job, involves encouraging students to learn about health, medicine, and science.

Careers described in this section include biomedical engineer, medical scientist, and research laboratory technician.

Biomedical Engineer

The Job Biomedical engineers apply engineering principles to solve medical and health-related problems. Biomedical engineering is a relatively new science, but already vast advances have been made in developing new cures and new machines for managing physical disorders.

Most engineers in this field are involved in research. They work with life scientists, chemists, and members of the medical profession to design and develop medical devices such as artificial hearts, pacemakers, dialysis machines, and lasers for surgery. Others work for private industry in the development, design, and sale of medical instruments and devices.

Biomedical engineers with computer expertise adapt computers to medical needs and design and build systems to modernize laboratory and clinical procedures. Some work for the National Aeronautics and Space Administration developing life support and medical monitoring systems for astronauts.

Many biomedical engineers teach and do research in colleges, universities, and medical colleges.

Places of Employment and Working Conditions Biomedical engineers work in industry, hospitals, pharmaceutical companies, and colleges and universities. Some phases of this work may be unpleasant when working with certain illnesses or medical conditions.

Qualifications, Education, and Training
The ability to think analytically, a capacity for details, and the ability to work as part of a team are all necessary. Good communication skills are important. Creativity is also vital to this field.

Mathematics and the sciences must be emphasized in high school. A bachelor's degree in engineering is the minimum requirement in this field. In a typical curriculum, the first two years are spent in the study of basic sciences such as physics and chemistry and mathematics, introductory engineering, and some liberal arts courses. The remaining years are usually devoted to specialized engineering courses. For this field that means a sound background in mechanical, electrical, industrial, or chemical engineering plus additional specialized biomedical training.

Engineering programs can last from four to six years. Those that require five or six years to complete may award a master's degree or may provide a cooperative plan of study plus practical work experience with a nearby industry.

All states require licensing of engineers whose work may affect life, health, or property or who offer their services to the public. Those who are licensed, about one-third of all engineers, are called registered engineers. Requirements for licensing include graduation from an accredited engineering school, four years of experience, and an examination.

Some biomedical engineers go on to earn their Ph.D. Advanced degrees are necessary for advancement and promotion, particularly in universities and medical centers.

Potential and Advancement
There are only about 4,000 biomedical engineers. Substantial growth is expected, but since the field is relatively small, few actual job openings will occur. Those with advanced degrees will have the best job opportunities.

Income
Starting salaries in private industry average $25,000 a year with a master's degree and up to $60,000 or more with a Ph.D.

Additional Sources of Information

Accreditation Board for Engineering and Technology
345 East 47th Street
New York, NY 10017

Alliance for Engineering in Medicine and Biology
1101 Connecticut Avenue, NW, Suite 700
Washington, DC 20036

American Society for Engineering Education
11 Dupont Circle, NW, Suite 200
Washington, DC 20036

Biomedical Engineering Society
P.O. Box 2399
Culver City, CA 90230

Junior Engineering and Technical Society (JETS)
1420 King Street, Suite 405
Alexandria, VA 22314

National Society of Professional Engineers
1420 King Street
Alexandria, VA 22314

Society of Women Engineers
345 East 47th Street, Room 305
New York, NY 10017

Medical Scientist

The Job   Medical scientists study causes and discover treatments for disease and other health problems. They often try to identify the kinds of changes in cells, chromosomes, or genes that signal the beginning of medical problems such as cancer or AIDS. Learning more about the physiological, immunological, pathological, and anatomical structures and changes that occur in organisms may provide clues for new cures, treatments, and drugs for the prevention and control of disease. Besides using basic research for new knowledge, medical scientists may reaffirm previous studies, examine results through new technology, and try to formulate new combinations of drugs to prevent and control illnesses.

Most medical scientists specialize in a specific area. These include anatomy, biochemistry, embryology, microbiology, pharmacology, and physiology. *Anatomists* study and examine the structure of organisms, from the cell to the formation of tissues and organs to the large structures of the human body. Many specialize in dissection, teaching, or use of electron microscopy. *Embryologists* study the development of a human from a fertilized egg through birth, and the causes of healthy and abnormal birth. This is a fast-growing field, due to the sociological crises of "test tube" babies, fertilization issues, cloning, abortion, birth defects, and increased drug usage (both pharmacological and recreational). The study of abnormal development of embryos and the causes of congenital malformations is called *teratology*.

Biochemists study the chemical composition of living things. They develop new understanding of complex chemical combinations involved in metabolism, reproduction, growth, and heredity.

Microbiologists study the relationship between bacteria, algae, viruses, and disease. They also investigate the effect of drugs (such as antibiotics) on bacteria and disease. Microbiologists use new technology to advance their understanding of cell reproduction and human disease. *Immunology* is a branch of microbiology that studies the human mechanisms that fight disease.

Physiologists study life functions, both in the human organism and at the cellular and molecular level, to learn more about normal and abnormal mechanisms. Physiologists may specialize in areas of reproduction, respiration, cardiology, neurology, growth, and movement.

Pharmacologists study the effects of drugs, chemicals, and other substances on humans and animals. Their research results indicate how drugs and chemicals act at the cellular level; how drugs can best be used; appropriate drug dosages; the effects of materials such as chemicals, pesticides, and poisons; and dangerous levels of chemicals.

In their laboratories, pharmacologists perform research using live animals and human tissues. Sometimes they inject chemicals, substances, or drugs into animals or culture them with live tissue samples. The goal of their research is to determine the effects of these substances on organs and body systems, and to identify any harmful side effects. Then, microbiologists can predict how useful a drug may be as a remedy for disease.

Places of Employment and Working Conditions   Most medical scientists work in research and development. Many experiments are conducted on laboratory animals. Most work in hospitals, testing laboratories, private industry, pharmaceutical or biotechnology establishments, colleges and universities, and medical and dental schools.

Medical scientists usually work regular hours in offices, laboratories, and institutes of higher learning. Scientists occasionally work long hours doing laboratory research experiments, examining data, and writing grant proposals. Strict safety procedures are followed, as some can work with dangerous organisms or toxic substances.

Qualifications, Education, and Training   For medical scientists, the Ph.D. degree is required for college teaching, graduate education, independent research, and for advancement to administrative positions. Sometimes a master's degree is sufficient for jobs as a research or laboratory assistant. Most colleges offer degrees in the biological sciences, and some offer advanced degrees. Some universities offer degrees in certain medical science areas such as anatomy, biochemistry, physiology, and microbiology. Medical schools sometimes offer Ph.D. degrees in medical sciences, and some also offer combined programs, earning both the Ph.D. and M.D. degrees. Medical scientists who administer drug or gene therapy to patients must have the M.D. degree.

The Ph.D. degree takes from four to six years to complete, following a bachelor's degree. Course work will include basic medical sciences, research techniques, and the successful completion of an original research project and doctoral dissertation written about the project.

In addition to the formal graduate education, medical scientists are usually expected to spend several years in a postdoctoral position before they are offered permanent positions. Postdoctoral work allows on-the-job training in a very specialized field of medicine or medical research. It also provides valuable laboratory experience, learning new technology and instrumentation. This learning experience provides additional skills and abilities that can be transferred to other research projects.

Potential and Advancement   Employment of medical scientists is expected to increase faster than the average for all occupations through the year 2005. Expected expansion in research related to health issues such as cancer and AIDS should result in growth. The main problem foreseen in the research and development field is the anticipated budget tightening of federal government agencies. Much medical research is funded by the federal government, and there may be smaller increases (even decreases) in the amount of grant money given to research, slowing the growth of the number of grants issued. Advancement in the field of medical sciences usually depends on education, postdoctoral fellowships, number of publications, and awards earned in teaching and research.

Income   Median annual income for medical scientists is about $37,500. Ten percent earn less than $16,500 (usually post-docs and beginning instructors), and 10 percent earn over $67,000. Annual income can exceed $100,000 for full professors, chairs of departments, and deans of medical colleges and universities.

In the federal government in 1995, microbiologists averaged $54,280; physiologists, $47,840; and geneticists, $60,110.

Additional Sources of Information

American College of Clinical Pharmacology
175 Strafford Avenue, Suite 1
Wayne, PA 19087

American Society for Pharmacology and Experimental Therapeutics
9650 Rockville Pike
Bethesda, MD 20814

American Physiological Society, Membership Services Dept.
9650 Rockville Pike
Bethesda, MD 20814

American Society for Biochemistry and Molecular Biology
9650 Rockville Pike
Bethesda, MD 20814

American Society for Microbiology, Office of Education and Training—
    Career information
1325 Massachusetts Avenue, NW
Washington, DC 20005

Research Laboratory Technician

The Job   Research laboratory technicians use the principles of science and mathematics to solve problems in specific areas of biomedical research. Their jobs are more practically oriented than those of biological and medical scientists. They set up, operate, and maintain laboratory instruments, set up experiments, make observations, calculate and record results, and sometimes develop conclusions.

As laboratory instrumentation and procedures have become more complex, the role of the technician has expanded. In addition to performing routine tasks under direction of the scientists, many technicians develop and adapt lab procedures to achieve better results, interpret data, and devise new solutions. Many use computers and computer-interfaced equipment.

Biomedical research laboratory technicians work with biological and medical scientists. They assist the scientists who conduct medical research, helping to expand our knowledge of cancer or AIDS, for example. Research laboratory technicians help develop medicinal and pharmaceutical preparations, analyze organic substances such as blood, food, and drugs, and use gene splicing and recombinant DNA techniques.

Places of Employment and Working Conditions   Research laboratory technicians work indoors in laboratories, and have regular working hours. Occasionally, some work irregular hours to monitor special experiments that can't be completed during regular working hours, or when a deadline must be met. Researchers in the biological or medical field sometimes work with disease-causing organisms or radioactive agents. Others work with laboratory animals, where there is always the possibility of bites and scratches. Safety procedures are strictly followed, however, and there are relatively few hazards.

Research laboratory technicians are employed primarily in research laboratories of faculty members at colleges, universities, and medical centers. Some are employed in hospital laboratories, private industry, and pharmaceutical companies.

Qualifications, Education, and Training   People interested in research and laboratory work need to have scientific ability and ability to work both independently and as a team member. They need to be highly responsible, honest, meticulous, and precise. Good oral and written communication skills are also valuable.

There are several different ways to qualify as a research technician. Some junior colleges offer two-year associate degrees in general science and mathematics. However, a bachelor's degree, with a major in biology or chemistry, is almost mandatory.

Besides formal education, much on-the-job training is required. Specific research techniques (such as culture techniques and gene cloning), complicated scientific equipment, various microscopes (such as transmission and scanning electron microscopes), and other laboratory procedures must be learned thoroughly. Applying the scientific method, creating new ways to approach scientific or medical problems, and analyzing data will all be necessary skills in a research laboratory.

135

Some research laboratory technicians go on to earn their master's degrees. Others, who are interested in teaching, as well as research, study for a Ph.D.

Potential and Advancement   Advancement in this field is primarily through experience and further education. The outlook for research laboratory technicians is better than average through the year 2005. The growing sophistication of biotechnological techniques, instrumentation, and equipment will influence growth. Due to a rather high turnover in this field, there will always be the need to replace technicians who retire or leave the profession. Most people who leave the field either go back to school for advanced degrees in research, apply to medical or other professional schools, or accept higher-paying jobs.

Income   Median annual earnings in 1994 for research laboratory technicians were about $26,900. Starting salaries are often in the $12,00 to $14,000 range. Income varies considerably with education and experience.

Additional Sources of Information

American Chemical Society
Educational Division, Career Publications
1155 16th Street, NW
Washington, DC 20036

Part II

How to Get and Keep a Job in Health Care

The Paperwork

The dreaded "paperwork"! Resumes. Cover letters. Application forms. Tests and licensing examinations. No one really likes to deal with the details of this aspect of job-hunting. Most people think of it as a hurdle, jumping through hoops, or just plain barriers to getting that job. But if you look at this task as something you only really have to do once, and that this chore is the doorway through which you can show your future employer your talents, it may make the process easier to tackle. Furthermore, once you get started, organize your thoughts and ideas, and start putting them down on paper, this duty doesn't seem quite so daunting.

Employers want to hire a person who is qualified and will do the job. Each "boss" will first learn about an applicant through his or her resume, cover letter, performance tests, and application forms. Only then can the employer determine who should get to the next step—the interview. Your job is to make the employer understand what education and abilities you have, so that he or she wants to meet and interview you in person. That is what the "paperwork" is all about. To create an advertisement about yourself. To get you in the door. Once you have completed all your "paperwork," the only thing you'll ever need to do again is revise it and update it on a regular basis. Let's take this task step by step.

Creating the Most Effective Resume

The resume is your calling card. It is an advertisement of your qualifications to a prospective employer. You can see this is vital to getting an interview. This is what you need to focus on: What do you need to say to cause the reader to want to meet you? You need to begin your resume writing with several steps. First, you need to review carefully your education, experiences, special abilities and skills, and other qualifications. Second, once you've gathered all the information, you need to put it all together in an eye-catching and organized manner.

To begin this process, you will need two different kinds of information: one, facts about yourself; and two, facts about the job you want. Let's begin.

Know Thyself   Start assembling information about yourself. Specific items appear on every resume. These are:

- *Current address and phone number.* If you are not home during the day, the best thing you can do is invest in an answering machine. Leave a simple and professional-sounding message, and check the tape every day. Return each message as soon as possible.
- *Career goals.* What kind of job are you seeking?
- *Work experience.* State every job held, place of employment, name and address of the employer, job title, and basic salary (optional).
- *Education.* Include each school's name, address, the years you attended, certificate or degree earned, and the course of study.
- *Special honors, awards, and recognition.* Be sure to include any special honors or recognition you received in your work experience or during your education.
- *Qualifications, skills, techniques.* Does the job description include particular skills that are needed for the job? Be sure to address these issues. Do you have computer knowledge? Do you type seventy words per minute? Do you know histological techniques, electron microscopy, how to run equipment in the laboratory? Don't be afraid to add specific skills that are not mentioned in the job description.
- *Specific abilities and attributes you possess for this particular job.* Does the job description require people skills? Are you particularly creative, well-organized, or very compassionate? Are you reliable, honest, and loyal? Are you a warm, caring, empathetic person? Are you a leader or a follower? Some personal attributes are very subjective, but spend some time considering how your abilities and attributes fit into the job.
- *Additional facts about yourself.* For example, do you play a musical instrument? This can demonstrate manual dexterity as well as musical ability. Do you run in marathon races? Endurance running can lead one to assume you have perseverance and dedication. Hobbies and interests outside of work can show the employer more about you as a person.

Know Thy Job   Start gathering information about the jobs and careers in which you are interested. You need to know the salary range, the education required, the experience required, and the schedule of working hours. You need to know the specific job duties. This knowledge can be used to customize your resume and cover letter for each prospective job. Review job announcements and study them to determine which qualifications are most important. Have a checklist of your qualities, qualifications, and specific skills and abilities, and refer to this list as you prepare for each job. Once you have gathered all this information, the next step is to form an easy-to-understand and attractive resume.

Putting It All Together
Now is the time to organize this information into an attractive package. This is creating the resume. There are some very important points to consider and keep in your mind while putting your resume together. Let's call these the ABCs of the resume. Here is what each letter, from A to P, refers to.

Action words. Use words with strong impact. Don't use the passive voice. For example, instead of just saying, "I did" or "I was responsible for," try saying, "I designed," "I implemented," or "I organized." These kinds of words suggest accomplishments and achievements. This is very important to the reader, who gets a sense of your actual involvement in your previous jobs and education. Other examples of action words are *researched, targeted, supervised, developed, created, directed, planned, increased, managed, wrote, analyzed,* and *presented.*

Brief. Your completed resume should be brief, preferably under two pages. The only exception to this rule is in academia. When applying for positions in academic institutions or research organizations, a resume is called a *curriculum vitae.* Writing a "CV" is a lot more detailed, and includes detailed descriptions of education, research grants, personal research programs, and published works. These documents can be twenty pages or longer! Generally speaking, however, you do not want to bore your future boss with an elaborate portrait of each and every job and volunteer project you have been involved in since you were in junior high school. Most employers looking for an employee do not want to read through a dissertation of your life.

In addition to having a brief resume, you need to write in short, concise sentences. Remember, minimum words, minimum length, minimum sentences. Just get the basic points across. If the employer wants more detail, he or she will ask for it.

Chronological. A chronological resume is probably the easiest to prepare. All information is presented according to time (for example, all jobs held since graduation from high school). Or you can proceed in a reverse chronological form, beginning with the present and ending at a specific point in time. This is very simple to understand, and is a good way to present educational data, as well as work experience.

Development. It is important to show how you have developed skills through your work and through your life experiences. This will demonstrate self-assessment and maturity.

Eye-catching. The resume must be inviting, forceful, and easily understood with just a glance. Make sure that the layout is pleasing. Use margins, proper spacing, headlines, outlining, and italics to present your information in a clear and interesting way. Remember that the resume is an advertisement for you, and must look good.

Functional. A second type of resume is the functional resume. It categorizes your work into specific areas of experience or skill that you would like to highlight. The functional resume stresses the specific areas of accomplishment that you feel are most marketable, and allows you to show professional growth. Most resumes utilize a combination of the chronological and functional formats. You may also target your resume to a specific job. You can accomplish this by simply changing your format slightly to include your job target and how your skills relate to that area. A functional description of your areas of expertise can follow the target section, with a chronological list of your education and work history following that.

Grammar. Your grammar should be perfect. Your typing, spelling, and punctuation should be perfect. Remember that this document represents *you.* If it looks sloppy and includes grammatical errors, this will reflect negatively on you.

Honesty. The principal of honesty is very simple. Never "fudge" anything. Be straightforward and honest about every piece of data you include on your resume.

Information. You must include basic information in your resume as outlined in the section "Know Thyself." Name, address, phone number, and current place of employment are essential facts. Also include an inventory of your skills and accomplishments, a work history, and education.

Job sought. Don't forget to include the exact job you are seeking. If you have targeted your resume, you will have already done this. If you are applying for a specific position, make sure the reader knows for which position you are applying. If you are not applying for a specific position, you should make this statement more general, so you'll be considered for a variety of positions.

Let's review and make sure you have covered the major points of the resume. Make sure you have demonstrated *knowledge* about yourself and the job market. Keep the *length* to one or two pages. Do not *misrepresent* yourself in any way. If you can't say something *nice,* don't say anything. For example, don't mention that you left your last job because your boss was a total idiot. Look over the finished product for proper *organization,* and finally, *proofread.*

After you have critiqued your resume for all these guidelines, take a final step—*edit.* Read everything carefully. Remove unnecessary words. Eliminate data that is not relevant. Correct spelling and grammatical errors. Give your resume to a number of people to read, and ask for feedback. They will catch things that you have missed. Be sure the layout is attractive. Finally, have your resume printed by a local printer on good quality paper. If you have access to a computer with a laser printer, you can buy your own quality paper and print your resume yourself. Use white, off-white, pale blue, or pale grey paper with a contrasting ink color. Remember, this is your calling card and you want to make a good first impression.

The Cover Letter

A cover letter is extremely important because it is your personal introduction to your potential employer. It encourages the employer to read your resume. Your resume lists your skills and experiences. Your cover letter relates those skills and experiences to your potential employer's specific needs. Every cover letter you write will have a slightly different slant as it relates your skills to that employer's needs. The cover letter must:

1. Arouse interest
2. Be a sales pitch to sell an employer on you
3. Contain snappy writing
4. Contain specific data
5. Close with a key point

Each letter must also be typed perfectly with dark, clear printing, on white or cream medium-weight bond paper. All cover letters should consist of a salutation, opening, body, and closing. Let's go through a letter point by point.

Salutation   Each letter should be addressed by name to the person with whom you wish to talk and who will do the hiring. Call the company to be sure you have the correct name and spelling. This will most likely be the person who will be supervising you on the job. Occasionally it might be a department head or someone in the personnel department. Sometimes someone in the personnel department screens the letters first, then sends them on to the specific person doing the hiring.

Opening   The opening needs to appeal to the reader and catch his or her attention. Remember, cover letters are sales letters. Talk about your interest in the company. Often, if you show sincere interest in a company, its representatives will feel the same in return. Mention the employer's recent awards or projects, or currently published complimentary comments. You can find such information in the business press, including local papers and magazines. Do your research. It will pay off. If you are answering an ad, mention it. If a specific person suggested that you write, use his or her name (always get the person's permission before doing this).

Body   The body of the letter should give a brief description of your qualifications for the job. Relate your skills and experiences to the job and company. Refer to your resume. Arouse the interest of the reader through

145

snappy writing consisting of some short and some long sentences. Reread this carefully. Does this section of the letter interest you so much that *you* want to meet you? Finally, get a second opinion from a trusted friend or advisor.

Closing   At the end of your cover letter, say that you want to meet with the recipient. Request an interview. Suggest dates and times you are available. Use a standard complimentary closing, such as "Sincerely" or "Sincerely yours." Leave three or four blank lines and then type your name. Don't forget to sign the letter above your typed name. If you are not using letterhead stationery that includes your phone number, be sure your phone number is typed under your name for easy reference.

The Application Form

There are a few large firms, some hospitals, clinics, and government agencies, who emphasize application forms more than resumes. These forms suit the style of the large organization because the employers feel that they can instantly find information if it always appears in the same place in the same way.

At first glance, the application form seems to give a job hunter no freedom of expression or leeway. These forms do not have the flexibility of the resume, but you can still find a way to use them to your best advantage. Remember, the attitude of the reader is, "Maybe this is the person we are looking for," not "Let's find out why this person is not qualified." Try to use each part of the form—experience blocks, education blocks, former employment blocks, skills blocks—to demonstrate that the person they are looking for is you!

Here are some general points to keep in mind while you are completing an application form:

1. *Application forms are actually a simple form of a resume.* If possible, create your resume before filling out any application forms. This will help you to spotlight your qualifications and serve as a reference tool when completing the application form.
2. *Request two copies of the form.* If you can get only one copy, photocopy it before you begin to fill it out. You'll need the extra copy to prepare a first draft.
3. *Read over the entire form before you start it.*

4. *If the same form is used by several divisions within the same organization, first prepare a master copy.* Photocopy it, and then add the specific job applied for, the date, and your signature. Complete that final step as you submit each photocopy to each division.
5. *Always type the form.* A typed form is much easier to read and looks much neater. If there are lots of very small spaces within the application, type the information, paste that paper onto the form, and then photocopy it.
6. *Never leave a blank.* When the reply requested does not apply to you, enter N/A for "not applicable." This lets the reader know that you did not simply skip over the question.
7. Always carry a resume and a copy of other frequently-asked-for information with you when visiting a potential employer. He or she may ask you to fill out an application form on the spot, and you will have all needed information at your fingertips. However, when possible, fill out the application at home and send it in with a cover letter and resume.
8. *Always be honest, direct, and correct with all information on an application form.*

Tests

A man with a violin case stood on a subway platform in the Bronx. He asked a conductor, "How do you get to Carnegie Hall?" The conductor replied, "Practice! Practice! Practice!"

That old joke holds good advice for people preparing for employment tests or interviews. The tests given to job applicants fall into four categories: general aptitude tests, practical tests, tests of physical agility, and medical examinations. You can practice for the first three. If the fourth is required, learn as soon as possible what the disqualifying conditions are, then have your physician examine you for them so that you do not spend years training for a job that you will not be allowed to hold.

To practice for a test, you must learn what the test is. Once again, you must know what job you want to apply for and for whom you want to work in order to find out what tests, if any, are required. Government agencies, which frequently rely on tests, will often provide a sample of the test they use. These samples can be helpful even if an employer uses a different test. Copies of standard government tests are usually available at the library.

If you practice beforehand, you'll be better prepared and less nervous on the day of the test. That will put you ahead of the competition. You will also improve your performance by following this advice:

- Make a list of what you will need at the test center, including several pencils; check it before leaving the house.
- Get a good night's sleep.
- Be at the test center early—at least 15 minutes early.
- Read the instructions carefully; make sure they do not differ from the samples you practiced with.
- Generally, speed counts; do not linger over difficult questions.
- Learn if guessing is penalized. Most tests are scored by counting up the right answers; guessing is all to the good. Some tests are scored by counting the right answers and deducting partial credit for wrong answers; blind guessing will lose you points—but if you can eliminate two wrong choices, a guess might still pay off.

The Interview

How Important Is the Interview?

The interview is probably the single most important step in your search for a job. No matter how attractive your resume, and how great your experiences and qualifications, all employers want to know who you are as a person. The purpose of the interview is twofold.

First, the employer wants to put a face to the name. He or she knows a lot about you from your cover letter, resume, and application. But what is most important to the interviewer is who you are as a human being. Are you friendly and likeable? Do you communicate easily? Can the employer visualize you in the position you have applied for? Do you want the job for the right reasons? These types of questions can only be answered through a face-to-face interview.

Second, the interview gives you a chance to visit the place of employment and meet the boss. An interview can be somewhat intimidating, and it's always reassuring to know that you, too, are making a decision. It is important to realize that the interview is rarely just a formality. The interview may "make you or break you"! But also recognize that *you* are interviewing the employer as well. Reminding yourself of this fact may help you relax during your interview. The interview also gives you a chance to check the place out. Don't be afraid to talk to other employees as you pass through the offices. Try to get a sense of the pervading atmosphere of the place. Do people seem happy there? Do they have a sense of camaraderie? Do workers have smiles on their faces or scowls? In order to have a healthy, happy job, you need a healthy and supportive environment in which to work. You don't want to accept a position, only to find yourself very unhappy and discouraged two months later.

Preparing for the Interview

The first step you should take in preparing for your interview is to *thoroughly research yourself*. Think about what your interviewer wants to know about you. Of course, he or she wants to know about your employment history, education, and job experience. Try to fill in the gaps where your resume leaves off. What are your most valued skills? Of what are you most proud? What goals have you set for yourself in the past few years? Have you accomplished those goals, and if so, how? What qualities do you possess that will help you do this job? What distinguishes you from the other applicants for this position? These are just a few sample questions that you should spend some time contemplating.

Another suggestion is to *write it down*. Spend some time answering these preceding questions. This exercise will help you put your thoughts in order. You will have some control over what you talk about in your interview. Be sure to have some topics ready about which you can fluently and articulately speak.

The second step is to *learn about the job and career for which you are applying*. You absolutely must have a little working knowledge about the tasks you will be required to do and the duties you will be performing. You must be able to explain how your experiences, qualifications, and education have prepared you for this job. It is also important to understand the company or institution for which you will be working. Check out some general information. How large is the company? How many people are employed there? Carefully look over any brochures or catalogues you have obtained. Write down everything you would like to know about. You may think you will remember these questions, but when your anxiety level begins to rise on your interview day, they might fly right out of your mind!

The third step in preparing yourself for an interview is to *practice*. This may sound silly, but it will help alleviate some of the anxiety you feel about the interview. Have a friend or relative sit down with you and practice talking about some of the ideas you have established about yourself or qualities you would like to demonstrate to the interviewer. Prepare a list of questions that may be asked in your interview. Have one of these people ask you some of the questions as if you were doing the real thing. Do this several times. It is amazing how fluent you become once you have organized your thoughts. Practice will not make you perfect, but you will gather insights about how you think on your feet. You will be more nervous, anxious, and trying harder to please during your actual interview. However, the more you talk, answer questions, and learn about yourself, the better you begin to know and understand yourself and your skills. Here are some commonly asked questions to get you started:

- Why are you applying for this job?
- What do you know about this company?
- Why should I hire you?
- Why do you want this position?
- What are your greatest strengths?
- What are your major weaknesses?

- What type of work do you like to do best?
- What would you do if… (some type of job-related crisis)?
- What are your interests outside work?
- What would you most like me to know about you?
- If I were talking to your best friend, what would he or she say about you?
- What other career choices or jobs have you explored?
- What challenges do you think you will face here?
- How did you hear about this job?
- What type of work do you like to do least?
- What did you like best (least) in your last job?
- How does your education and experience relate to this job?
- What are your short-term goals?
- Where do you see yourself in the next five (ten) years?
- How would you describe yourself?
- Were you ever fired? Why?
- What are your salary requirements?

The more you think about these questions, the easier it will be to answer them on the spot during an interview.

Interview Essentials

The day of your interview has finally arrived! You are tense and nervous. What should you do? Taking a shower will relax you and you will be fresh and ready. Look in the mirror and say out loud, "I have a lot to offer! I am great! I look great!" (or will, after you shave, put on makeup, or whatever you need to do!). Put yourself in a positive frame of mind. Be confident!

Should you eat before your interview? Yes! If you are not hungry due to anxiety, just have a small glass of juice and a piece of toast. Do not load up on coffee. You will be wired enough without it. You don't want to add to the shakes you already may have, or ask to use the restroom the moment you sit down.

Your appearance is important. You need to look fresh, clean, and professional. Don't overdo makeup and jewelry. Make sure your hair is neat and trimmed. Look the part of the job. First impressions are very important.

Be sure to leave your home in plenty of time in case you get lost or something unexpected happens. Also, bring extra copies of your resume with you, and add any updated information in case the interviewer asks for it. Here is a small list of cardinal rules that I feel are *essential* to follow during your interview day:

1. Be on time
2. Be honest and ethical
3. Know yourself and maximize your strengths
4. Be courteous, respectful, and friendly
5. Show sincere interest in the job and place of employment

Your interviewer, whoever he or she may be, deserves your respect. Address your interviewer as "Dr.," "Mr.," "Mrs.," or "Ms." If you're not sure about this, ask.

When your interviewer, or the secretary, calls your name, respond immediately. Look directly into the eyes of your interviewer. As you are being introduced, offer your hand in a hearty handshake. Be firm and confident, not lifeless or bone-crushing. I personally dislike shaking a hand that does not respond. This is very important for both men and women—you need to grow comfortable with offering your hand in a firm handshake.

As you step into your interviewer's office, take a deep breath and take the seat offered to you. Try to relax and be yourself. Remember, you have practiced and prepared. This is it.

Your interview will be a conversation between two people. However, the interview will differ from a casual conversation in that it has a distinct purpose, clear goals, and a set plan. Your interviewer will be fulfilling two tasks: 1) observing everything about you and 2) asking questions to learn as much as he or she can about you. Your job will be 1) to answer all questions straightforwardly and honestly, and 2) to find out information about the job and company.

There are three very important things *not* to do in an interview. These are:

1. Do not falsify any data or misrepresent yourself in any way.
2. Do not make excuses for yourself—be straightforward and don't be afraid to admit past mistakes. No one wants to hear a long explanation on why you were fired from a particular job or why you failed a course in school. Short and simple is the key.
3. Do not be afraid to ask questions. Remember that the interview is a two-way street. You really do need to learn as much as you can about the job, to see if it is the job you want! You, too, need to make a knowledgeable decision.

Here are some sample questions you might wish to ask an interviewer:

- What would a day on this job entail?
- To whom would I report? May I meet this person?
- Would I work with anyone? May I meet them?

- Would I supervise anyone? May I meet them?
- How important is this job to the company?
- Can I advance in this company? How?
- Why did the last person leave this job?
- Will I be evaluated on a regular basis? How often and by whom?
- What do you see as the greatest challenge in this position?
- Is this company growing or downsizing?

Listen to the interviewer's answers carefully. Don't be afraid to get down to specifics. You may have noticed that a question about salary and fringe benefits is not on the list. Your focus at the first interview should be on the job and the company, not on the salary and fringe benefits. Once you have been offered the position, you can negotiate the salary and request information on the fringe benefits.

Interview Follow-up

Be sure to thank the interviewer for his or her time, and make sure you understand the next step of the process. Will the interviewer contact you? Does he or she need more information or reference names? Always end on a positive note by reaffirming your interest in the position and making a last point of why you are the person to fill that job opening.

Write a thank-you note, and if you are truly interested in the position, say so. Explain your interest and why you are the perfect person for the job. Be sure you include your address and phone numbers in your letter.

If the interviewer said he or she would get back to you in a week, and two weeks have passed with no contact, call the office and simply ask if he or she has made a decision. It is always important to keep the lines of communication open.

Health Careers in the 21st Century

The one absolute in the health care industry is that it will change. You will continually face hiring freezes, mass layoffs, increasing technology, elimination of jobs and workers, and variations in the economy. The days of working at one job, with one employer, with one or two specific tasks are over! The last few years of the nineties will bring continued restructuring of the institutions we know and understand today.

Furthermore, there is no such thing as the perfect job or career. In order to prepare yourself for changes, promotions, and new career opportunities in health care, you must take control of your career, empower yourself, and manage your own destiny. No one will do this for you. You must be prepared for the turbulence of the health career market today and tomorrow. How can you equip yourself to do this? Read on.

Preparing for Your Future

As you gain employment in the health care field, you need to be constantly thinking about how you can further that career. Sometimes there may be opportunities to move upward. A supervisor may be promoted, leaving a door open for you to pursue that step up. Other opportunities may be sideways, but can offer chances to grow and expand your skills. You must keep this in the back of your mind at all times. Here are some ways to improve yourself and your marketability.

Acquire New Skills   Always take the opportunity to improve your skills and abilities. You can do this by attending seminars when they are offered or taking courses through your organization, vocational schools, apprenticeship programs, community colleges, or universities. You can also go as far as obtaining additional certifications or degrees. Look into the possibilities of the company paying for continuing education. Approach your boss and say, "I'm interested in learning" and give him or her a brochure or announcement of the course you want to attend. Organizations often have a budget for educational activities. Don't be afraid to ask. Next, constantly evaluate yourself and determine what areas in your work life need improvement. Observe changes that are occurring in your company. Who is getting promoted? Why? What is he or she doing that you are not? Once you've determined where you want to go and what skills you need to develop, do it. Don't procrastinate. The more knowledge and abilities you possess, the more valuable you will be to an employer.

Keep Records

Document, document, document! Photocopy everything. Make copies of all correspondence. Purchase and keep file folders where you place letters, evaluations, and notes. We often make the big mistake of thinking that our boss, supervisor, or company knows and keeps track of everything we do. This is a fallacy. You must remind management how valuable you are. You can do this by careful documentation. The ideal, of course, would be to keep a daily journal. Time, however, does not often permit this. But do pick a time (weekly, monthly, annually) to write down your accomplishments, salary changes, changes in benefits, promotions, awards, successes, and failures. Don't forget to include improvements you've made in the job and how you did it. Keep account of the seminars and educational opportunities you have pursued. Once you've done this, type it into a document. Make copies and send it to your supervisor, and to his or her boss or the head of the department if appropriate, and keep a copy for yourself. In this way, you can be assured that everyone of importance knows your importance to the company.

Be Flexible

It is always crucial to keep your options open. Be aware of new opportunities in the job market. Keep up with advancements in your field. Periodically review your skills and abilities and reexamine your interests and goals. These will change as you change. As you grow and mature in your career, you may realize that the fascination you felt for an area in health care has diminished. A fire may be lit under you to pursue another area. You may find you have developed skills you never thought were possible. New technology may be eliminating your job. Continually set new goals for yourself and keep your options open. Keep your eye on the future and make yourself aware of what's happening in your particular field and your particular company. Ignorance is never an excuse. Remember, *you are in charge of your own career!*

Keep Track of New Skills

We all possess different kinds of skills and abilities. There are job-related skills that take specific training. "Experience" skills are obtained through maturity and experience. You are not specifically trained with these skills, but you learn them through your daily job, from other people, or through your own maturing process. When you evaluate yourself periodically, keep these experience skills in mind and document them. For example, previously you may have hated public speaking. But by losing some self-consciousness and practicing through job presentations and reporting to committees, this now may be one of your strong suits.

Consider "transfer" skills as well. These are skills that can be used anywhere, and are not job-specific. Transfer skills can be "transferred" from one job to another. Try to discover common links and similarities of job characteristics between your current career and your next goal.

Keep Up-to-Date   It is of utmost importance to keep up-to-date in your health care field. To do this, you must read. Read about advances in technology. Read journals in your area of expertise. Be aware of the latest research. A great way to keep abreast of current events is to regularly attend local, regional, and national meetings in your field. Once again, funds are often available for this in health care organizations. Your employer should be delighted that you wish to attend these meetings, and may pay for the registration fee, and possibly transportation costs as well. Become a member of the local, regional, and national societies in your field (such as the American Dental Association or the Association of Emergency Medical Technicians, for example). By becoming a member, you will receive journals or newsletters, notices of meetings, lectures, and seminars, and ads for educational opportunities. You will find this information extremely useful. Attending these meetings will also help you to network with colleagues in your field, others in similar fields, and job and education opportunities.

Take Charge of Your Future   Let's review the importance of being in control of your future in the health care industry.

- Empower yourself through knowledge of yourself, your field, your skills, and available opportunities.
- Be realistic about your abilities, interests, and goals.
- Accept change and learn to like it.
- Learn to create your own opportunities through networking, positive actions, documentation, and research.

Growth Areas of the Future

Certain areas in the health care industry will definitely grow in the 21st century. These areas include primary health care services, home health care, outpatient services, medical technology, and networking amongst all factions of health care.

Primary Care

With the availability of health care, the access to public and private health insurance, and the improved interest in prevention, the need for providers of nonspecialized health care is increasing. Specific areas of need include practitioners who are not physicians, but can provide initial services. The need for nonphysician caregivers such as physician assistants and nurse practitioners should increase tremendously as we enter the 21st century.

Home Health Care

The changes in physician reimbursement and health insurance are leading to decreased patient hospitalization. One of the fastest-growing industries is that of home health care services.

Outpatient Services

Medical services that used to require week-long stays, such as various surgeries and medical procedures and testing, are now being performed in outpatient departments, clinics, and even in physicians' offices.

Technology

Occupations will continue to emerge as advances continue to be made in biomedical technology. Growth in the health professions will proceed as new laboratory procedures develop and as new diagnostic techniques are discovered. The 21st century may lead to new treatments, if not cures, for cancer, AIDS, and other debilitating diseases.

Networking

Significant progress will be made in health care networking. New computer technology and new Internet systems will provide vast increases in networking between care providers. New computer programming will change many areas of health and diagnostics. Significant combining of physicians' medical practices and of business and medical knowledge will provide new jobs and the need for new areas of expertise.